MW01286454

The Third Unconscious

The Third Unconscious

The Psycho-sphere in the Viral Age

Franco 'Bifo' Berardi

VERSO

London • New York

To Federico Campagna,
the hidden instigator of this book

First published by Verso 2021
© Franco Berardi 2021

1 3 5 7 9 10 8 6 4 2

Verso
UK: 6 Meard Street, London W1F 0EG
US: 20 Jay Street, Suite 1010, Brooklyn, NY 11201
versobooks.com

Verso is the imprint of New Left Books

ISBN-13: 978-1-83976-253-6
ISBN-13: 978-1-83976-254-3 (UK EBK)
ISBN-13: 978-1-83976-255-0 (US EBK)

British Library Cataloguing in Publication Data
A catalogue record for this book is available from the British Library

Library of Congress Cataloging-in-Publication Data
A catalog record for this book is available from the Library of Congress

Typeset in Sabon by MJ & N Gavan, Truro, Cornwall
Printed and bound by CPI Group (UK) Ltd, Croydon CR0 4YY

Contents

Preface

This book explores the ongoing mutation of the social Unconscious. My point of observation is that which we inhabit at present: the historical threshold marked by the viral pandemic and by the catastrophic collapse of capitalism. From this threshold, we can see ahead of us a horizon of chaos, exhaustion and tendential extinction.

This mutation is perfectly summarised by the Japanese philosopher Sabu Kosho. In his book *Radiation and Revolution* (2020), Kosho writes with hopeless clarity: 'Philosophically, this is an ontological shift from dialectics to immanence – from totalization by capitalism and by the state to the omnipresence of singular events. In this shift lies the prospect of planetary revolution to be grasped in the *decomposition of the World* and the *rediscovery of the Earth*.'

The concepts that emerge in Sabu Kosho's understanding of the Fukushima 2011 apocalypses are key for interpreting the global apocalypses of 2020: the ubiquitous, unstoppable proliferation of the principle of dissolution (radiation, viruses), the erosion of all symbolic and political orders, and the comeback of the long-denied Earth. *Terra*, defined by Deleuze and Guattari as *the great deterritorialised*, is reasserting itself and sweeping away the pathetic power of politics with the force of tsunamis, wildfires, viral epidemics.

I think that philosophy and psychoanalysis, far from panicking, far from railing against chaos, should assume the horizon of chaos and of exhaustion as a starting point for their reflection. Everything needs to be redefined, particularly what takes place in the intimate space of desire, emotion, fear.

The Unconscious is a realm without history, with no sequentiality, no before and after: it would be impossible to write a 'History of the Unconscious'. But it is possible to describe a history of the psycho-sphere of a society, and, in this sense, it is possible to speak of a 'third' Unconscious: the third form taken by the Unconscious within the late modern mental environment.

The 'first' phase was explored by Freud, who conceived the Unconscious as the dark side of the well-ordered framework of Rational Progress.

Science, education, industriousness were the pillars of modern public life. Marriage, monogamy and nuclear family were the pillars of modern private life.

In *Civilization and Its Discontents* (1930), Freud asserted that social normality demands a high degree of denial of desire or repression of *Trieb* (sexual drive and instinctuality). The bourgeois form of 'normality' dominant in the early twentieth century produced a particular form of suffering that Freud called 'neurosis'. To run the daily business of life, the modern individual was obliged to renounce, to repress, and possibly to forget their own sexual drives – and this removal was pathogenic. Neurosis was the general form of this pathology.

The framework changed in the last decades of the twentieth century, when the acceleration of the info-sphere and the intensification of the nervous stimulation (internet communication and cultural globalisation) jeopardised the systemic repression of desire and the psychopathological regime of neurosis.

The first intuition of this transformation of the psycho-cultural landscape can be found in Deleuze and Guattari's *Anti-Oedipus*, the book that marked the shift from structuralism to creative-rhizomatic thought but also the book that

conceptually opened a Pandora's box of desire, thus anticipating the neoliberal hypermobilisation of desire's energy as
disjoined from pleasure.

In *Anti-Oedipus*, Deleuze and Guattari reject the idea that
the Unconscious is a sort of depository of the experiences
that we don't want to see, or to remember, or to bring into
our conscious life. The Unconscious is not a theatre, but it
is a laboratory: the unconscious is the magmatic force that
ceaselessly brings about new possibilities of imagination and
experience.

Today, fifty years after the publication of *Anti-Oedipus*, we
can read the creative thought of Deleuze and Guattari as the
ambiguous (extremely ambiguous, and extremely rich) cast
for a double-edged future: the utopian future of the 'liberation
of desire' and the dystopian future of neoliberal capitalism,
where desire is celebrated as the impulse of consumption, competition and economic growth, while pleasure is constantly
postponed.

The entire media system has been mobilised to expand
on the promises of enjoyment, but this acceleration of the
information-flow has overloaded the capacity of human attention, thus ever postponing the possibility of pleasure, which
has ultimately become unattainable. This social regime has
led to the configuration of a new psychopathological regime,
which has characterised the past few decades: the age of panic,
depression and, ultimately, psychosis.

Panic means perception of the excess of possibility, intuition of an inaccessible amount of pleasure. A person panics
because they are in view of an excess of pleasure that they
cannot actually experience. Panic is a line of escape from
depression, and depression is the reassuring comeback from a
panicking trip. This is the inner oscillation of the postneurotic
psycho-sphere.

In the age of the Second Unconscious, neurosis is no longer
the general mode of psychic suffering. As the explosion of the

unconscious leads to a condition of nervous hyperstimulation and psychological frustration, psychosis takes the place of neurosis.

The rhizomatic whirlwind of the networked experience drags the unconscious, which Freud defines as *Innere Ausland* (the intimate foreign land), out of itself, externalising it to the point of a psychotic explosion.

I call 'semiocapitalism' this linkage of accumulation, semiotic production and nervous stimulation.

Guattari suggests that schizophrenia has to be considered as a condition of the free production of meaning. In his thought, the schizoid becomes the crucial figure of an adventure of liberation, creativity and knowledge. But this is only the liberating side of the acceleration. There is another side to it, which was denounced by Jean Baudrillard in *Symbolic Exchange and Death* (1976): the breathtaking acceleration of nervous stimulation (seduction, simulation, hyperreality) goes hand in hand with neoliberal globalisation, provoking a disturbance in the sphere of experience.

The psychopathology of semiocapitalism is marked by anxiety, attention disorders and panic. Depression comes as the final symptom of the semiocapitalist regime: the intensity of the social and emotional rhythm becomes unbearable, and the only way to escape suffering is to sever the link with desire, and, consequently, also the desiring link with reality.

Today, in the third decade of the new century, the phase of the Second Unconscious appears to be coming to a close. We are entering, it seems, a new psycho-sphere where a Third Unconscious is beginning to take shape. Beware: the shape of this new realm of the Unconscious is not easily definable; nor is it predictable, because the evolution of the psycho-sphere is not linear. There is no determinism in the psycho-sphere; there is no map of the *Innere Ausland* because, as Freud asserts, the Unconscious has no consistency and no logic. So we cannot know exactly in what direction(s) the mental-scape will evolve, what kind of evolution(s) the Covid-19 pandemic will cause, as it converges with a widespread economic and social collapse.

When I speak of the Third age of the Unconscious, I refer to an open future that will be shaped by our consciousness, by our political action, by our poetic imagination, and by the therapeutic activity that we'll be able to develop during this transition. Despite these necessary caveats, it is already possible to outline at least some of the conditions of the current psycho-shift.

The threshold is here, it is now: it emerged with the arrival of coronavirus in the space of our collective awareness. This bio-info-psycho virus is changing irreversibly our social proxemics, our affective expectations, our unconscious. Although the lines of this ongoing mutation are still blurred, some of its general traits are already clear and within our range of vision. First, the proximity of bodies has become a problematic factor, and its survival as part of our social life is increasingly endangered. Second, the spread of suffering in the pandemic age (not only medical suffering but also economic suffering, social suffering, and ultimately mental suffering) is already growing so intolerable that a form of immunisation against emotion may become dominant: autism and alexithymia might enter the fray of the psycho-sphere as the internalisation of the refusal to feel the emotions of others, and possibly also one's own emotions. What I describe in this book is not a well-outlined path of mutation but a magmatic field of possibility, in a landscape of anxiety.

In the first part of this book, 'On the Threshold', I will describe the effects of the irruption of the coronavirus into the space of collective sensibility and collective imagination.

In the second part, 'The Imminent Psycho-Sphere', I will try to ponder the different (even diverging) trends that are inscribed within the ongoing psychological mutation, as it affects the spheres of sexuality, social proxemics and desire.

In the third and last part, 'Becoming Nothing', I will outline the landscape of this century as it appears to me from the standpoint of the present: a world that has grown old, the exhaustion of both physical and nervous resources, extinction as the direction of our time. Only a new movement of imagination could possibly dispel this horizon of probability.

If this is the new horizon of the Unconscious, however, we should remember again that the Unconscious is not a deposit, but a laboratory. The most urgent question is not what the Unconscious perceives or projects out of itself. The question is: How will the Third Unconscious find a way out of its own nightmares?

Part I

On the Threshold

Threshold/Poetry

A novel coauthored by William S. Burroughs and Philip K. Dick does not exist. The British director Ridley Scott mixed their literary destinies when he used the title of a short novel written by Burroughs – *Blade Runner (a Movie)*, 1979 – as the title for *Blade Runner* (1982), based on Dick's *Do Androids Dream of Electric Sheep?* (1968).

The movie that constituted the pinnacle of aesthetic consciousness of the techno-cultural mutation underway in the 1980s emerged at the meeting point between Burroughs's and Dick's imaginations.

The topic of Burroughs's short novel is that of a strange epidemic of contagious cancer. The setting is today's world. After riots in 1984, at the end of the twentieth century a new disease emerges and rapidly begins to spread. This blitz-cancer is a fatal disease, but it is also capable of endowing its host (always a man, since women do not exist in Burroughs's imaginary) with enormous sexual energy. Although medical institutions have forbidden its diffusion, the blitz-cancer circulates through the city in the hands of the blade runners, who carry it around alongside other drugs and antidotes. Burroughs's *Blade Runner* was a delirious text, and despite the movie it still remains almost unknown to the general public.

This delirium also contained an intuition that was reproposed in Burroughs's *Ah Pook Is Here* (likewise published in 1979): language as a form of viral infection and the virus as the prime metaphor of that mutation which we call 'culture'. *Ah Pook* ends with an apocalyptic vision.

In Burroughs, language may be seen as a virus that in ancient times stabilised itself inside the organism of the human animal, pervading it, mutating it, and transforming it into what it is now.

In *The Ticket That Exploded* he writes, 'Modern man has lost the option of silence. Try to stop your internal sub-vocal discourse. Try to achieve even ten seconds of interior silence. You will encounter a resisting organism that *forces you to talk* … Language is a genetic defect with no immunology.'[1]

The origins of culture, Burroughs says, can be found in an infection of the mind and of the environment. Then we may argue that the shift from nature to the cultural condition is enabled by a viral infection. This virus provoked a schizoid effect: an inclination to build fictitious universes that do not correspond to the immediate perceptual experience but convey a linguistic architecture of meaning whose foundation is nowhere to be found, because it is only the projection of a world of language on the screen of outer reality.

Also the Italian philosopher Paolo Virno, in his 2013 book on negation, *Saggio Sulla Negazione*, suggests that language acted as the evolutionary jump that established the quest for meaning – thus setting in motion the endless chain of misunderstandings, contradictions, differentiations, conflicts and wars.[2]

Burroughs writes, 'We have observed that most of the trouble in the world has been caused by ten to twenty percent of folks who can't mind their own business, because they have no business of their own to mind, any more than a smallpox virus. Now your virus is an obligate cellular parasite and my contention is that evil is quite literally a virus parasite occupying a certain brain area which we may term the RIGHT center.'[3]

And also:

In these caves the white settlers contracted a virus passed down along their cursed generations that was to make them what they are today a hideous threat to life on the planet. This virus this ancient parasite is what Freud calls the unconscious spawned in the caves of Europe on flesh already diseased from radiation. Anyone descended from this line is basically different from those who have not had the cave experience and contracted this deadly sickness that lives in your blood and bones and nerves that lives where you used to live before your ancestors crawled into their filthy caves. When they came out of the caves they couldn't mind their own business. They had no business of their own to mind because they didn't belong to themselves any more. They belonged to the virus. They had to kill torture conquer enslave degrade as a mad dog has to bite. At Hiroshima all was lost.[4]

Language is the viral agent that enables the schizophrenic separation of conscious experience from biological nature, while at the same time secreting the unconscious; that innermost, foreign subtalk which we can never fully master and that often takes the upper hand in our social behaviours.

The linguistic virus has a schimogenic effect because it ushers in a second world, diverging from what is immediately present: the cultural universe is a schism from nature, a creation that is intimately self-contradictory.

If Burroughs's architecture is essentially schizophrenic, it is also perfectly complementary with the paranoid architecture of Philip Dick.

Burroughs imagines a dystopian metropolis of sickness and toxicity where couriers incessantly circulate drugs along the streets and along media channels, keeping the nervous system in a permanent state of excitement and fear: electronic adrenaline.

This Burroughsian nightmare sounds almost like a description of the planet after the end of the coronavirus pandemic and of the time of lockdowns: medicalisation of every fragment of the economic system and bankruptcy of the financial institutes and political institutions.

Any comeback to the normal world seems impossible, as we jump into a dimension where pandemic danger becomes the core of the economy and of political rule. Burroughs again: 'I advance the theory that in the electronic revolution a virus *is* a very small unit of word and image ... Unloosing this virus from the word could be more deadly than unleashing the power of the atom. Because all hate, all pain, all fear, all lust is contained in the word.'[5]

What can we expect after the spread of the virus and after the wide medicalisation of life? A planetary war among the big corporations of biological research and the political institutions, or the contrary, a holy alliance of biogenetic engineers and big finance?

Little by little, we are shifting from Burroughs's exploded universe to the concentrationary universe of Philip Dick. The advertising system is in ruins because advertisement sells a world that is no longer accessible – consequently, techno-mediatic production migrates towards the creation of simulated stimulation machines. The synthetic techno-maya secretes a social life of its own: social distancing becomes the rule that commands a remote form of the economy and of the daily business of life.

The technology of virtual reality, first promoted in the 1980s by Jaron Lanier, then forgotten in the wake of the network euphoria, has been recently relaunched by Oculus Rift – and, in the near future, it may also stick its tentacles inside the global mind, injecting growing doses of Synaesthetic Simulated Life.

The 5G technology for cellular communication networks will multiply their transmission capacity so that individuals will be able to transfer more and more actions from the offline to the online dimension. At the same time, however, this enhancement of broadband connectivity will improve the performance of those devices for total control that are based on the (growing) amount of data extracted from the social environment.

Eventually, the recent lockdowns might appear as an early experimentation with a new form of life. A life in which bodily contact is reduced to a minimum, if it is not abolished, while centralised control on the activity of the individuals is established as a preventive measure against the spreading of pandemics – and therefore as a postponement of the impending extinction of humankind, or at least of human civilisations.

A crucial topic in Dick's overwhelming and chaotic oeuvre is the threat of an invasion of the mental environment in which we dwell. Such invasion can be exogenous or endogenous: it can be provoked by external agents like the drug D in *A Scanner Darkly* or like the *kipple* that returns many times in Dick's novels. It can also be generated inside the organic mind, like the psychosis that he often writes about.

Dick was diagnosed with schizophrenia at the age of nineteen, and the subject of psychosis is recurrent throughout his work.

In schizophrenia, the *idios kosmos* (private world) broadens enormously, to the point of integrating the system of relations and meanings of the *koinos kosmos* (shared world). The schizophrenic person recomposes the fragments of reality that belong to their mind, by creating their own principles of organisation.

The *koinos kosmos* is the world where we act and move every day (or: where we believe we are acting and moving). The sphere of social, economic affective exchanges that we call 'reality' can be distinguished from the *idios kosmos* that we create inside our mind and that from our mind is projected outside.

Some psychiatrists view schizophrenia as a form of overinclusion within the signification process. When we open too many lines of semantic flight, when we attribute too many meanings to the signs that we receive, when the surrounding environment seems overloaded with messages that we must decode, our existence can turn difficult and painful and can grow so chaotic that our mind feels on the brink of explosion.

Somehow, however, mental activity itself could be considered as an invading agent, as an alien who is living within us. Ignorance – the fact that we do not know something that is concerning us in an extremely intimate way – can also be an invader.

In a 1982 interview in which he discusses Rachael, the beautiful replicant of *Do Androids Dream of Electric Sheep?*, Dick suggests that Rachael is an android who does not know that she is.

The idea that all of us may be aliens without knowing it opens very large philosophical and psychological perspectives.

Since the human being is the product (cultural, technical, historical) of countless influences, impulses and implementations, we may infer that it is an android who wrongly believes itself to be a human. And also what is the meaning of this word: *itself*? What is this 'self-ness' if not the inner gaze of a biological organism that is technically and culturally modified so that it believes himself not to be an object but, simply, a 'self'?

Just Imagine for a Moment

Just imagine for a moment if Burroughs and Dick had actually managed to write a novel together. I guess they would have described something similar to what we are going through right now in 2020 and 2021: the proliferation of a bio-info-psycho virus inside a society that is on the brink of an environmental, financial, but also psychic collapse.

Global society has not entered a difficult situation because of the explosion of the coronavirus epidemic. It was already on the edge of collapse. Let's not forget that important point.

This is immediately clear, if we consider the environmental disasters that plagued the year 2019 alone: the gigantic fires of Australia, Siberia, California and Amazonia; the melting ice in Greenland and the broader Arctic; the foggy nightmare of Delhi; and the invasions of locusts in Africa are evidence that climate change is already deploying its deadly effects. The months immediately preceding the spread of the virus were also marked by a social spasm, a proliferation of huge demonstrations and riots from Hong Kong to Santiago, to Quito, Beirut, Paris, Barcelona and Tehran. The global economy was already miring in a long stagnation, counting for its survival on the ceaseless injection of financial investments, paid through the impoverishment of social life and infrastructures. A psychic collapse, too, was clearly perceivable in social and political behaviour, such as the revengeful choices of many electorates worldwide. The sense of an impending catastrophe was already palpable.

The artistic landscape of 2019, particularly in film, was punctuated by flashes of apocalyptic consciousness. Just before the explosion of the virus, the sensitive antennae of many artists were perceiving a sort of pathological vibration. Ken Loach's movie *Sorry We Missed You* portrays working conditions in which a psychic collapse becomes inevitable. Todd Phillips's *Joker* recounts the spread of mental suffering in a society that is prone to forms of psychotic rebellion. Bong Joon-ho's *Parasite* goes through the stages of a frantic struggle to survive, in a world where everybody fights everybody else, while every social stratum crushes and oppresses the strata below – until an epidemic of violence comes to destroy all kinds of hierarchy.

Society before the pandemic was already a collapsing society: it was at that point when a bio-semiotic agent came to bring about a major disruption, paralysis and silence.

This is how mutations happen: starting from events that are inconsistent and incompatible with the previous context and that cannot be interpreted in rational terms. Nonsignifying units of enunciation set in motion profound and irreversible changes that we cannot oppose, that politics cannot control, and that power has no weapons to destroy.

This mutation has in itself the elements of a novel by Philip Dick, but it deploys them along the conceptual lines of William Burroughs.

The virus acts as a recoder: first of all, it recodes the immune system of the individuals, and then of entire populations. But the virus's operations overflow the biological sphere into the psycho-sphere, through the effects of fear and distancing. The virus transforms the reactions of a body to the body of the other, thus reframing the sexual unconscious.

We have already seen this process in the years of the immuno-deficiency syndrome that deeply affected the erotic sphere, but to a certain extent endangered the very dimension of social solidarity.

Finally, we have a media-spread of the virus: information is saturated by the epidemics; public attention is captured and totalised. But at the same time, a new sensibility can also emerge: the past is perceived in a different way, and the future is upturned. The past of perpetual connection will soon appear in our memory as a symptom of loneliness and anxiety, and the online dimension will be unconsciously internalised as a feature of sickness.

An Immense Schismogenetic Poem

This bio-info-psycho circuit must be processed and aesthet-ically elaborated to outline some cognitive modalities that might enable us to pass beyond the threshold where we find ourselves at present.

The threshold is a passage from light to darkness.

But it may be also a passage from darkness to light.

The threshold is the point where, according to Gregory Bateson, a schismogenetic process can begin. Not a revolution, not a new political order, but the emergence of a new organism that is different from the old organism.

An activity of collective elaboration is needed, if we wish to avoid that this schismogenetic process will happen too painfully. And this activity will have to deal with signs, linguistic gestures, subliminal suggestions, subconscious convergences.

This is, properly speaking, the space of poetry: the activity that shapes new dispositions of sensibility.

I have the impression that a poetic explosion is underway in a fragmentary, sporadic, disseminating, rhizomatic manner all along the circuits of the internet. Despite our criticism over the past few years, on this occasion the internet is also showing a potency of solidarity and sublimation.

I know that the prevailing transformation enabled by the digital network on human communication is pathological and ferocious. I can see the rationale of Salman Rushdie's meditations in his baroque surrealistic novel *Quichotte*, where he distinguishes between a B.G. (Before Google) age and our age: 'Our age, A.G. [After Google], in which the mob rules, and the smartphone rules the mob.'[6]

Nevertheless, there are signals in the all-encompassing global flow, hinting towards a virtuous change. A more refined shape of communication seems to be emerging. It's obvious: people have more time, they cannot even go to cafés and talk with friends, so they stay in front of the computer and they digitise. Rather: they no longer merely digitise; they write. A wide process of therapeutic and creative writing is traversing the overwhelming noise of the hypernet.

Countless conscious and sensitive netters are pondering the ways to recount a microscopic event happening in their neighbourhood, and they try to elaborate some enormous event they have watched on TV. Millions of people are recording fragments of their time on the threshold – they make small movies, they use images and words to express their own experience. They are weaving the fabric of the emergent cosmos that may become recognisable beyond the threshold: that new cosmos which is already schismogenetically diverging from the dying form of the old cosmos, from the chaotic trap of the rules that used to hold the world together by destroying it.

A collective search is taking place on an enormous scale, a search that is simultaneously psychoanalytical, political, aesthetic and poetic.

During the pandemic, we have experienced a deep laceration in the meaning of action, production and life. This is not only a medical subject: the very foundations of the civilisation which we inherited (which we have suffered but have also enjoyed) are in question.

When this is over, will we continue to accept financial cuts to public spending? Will we continue to accept the pollution that makes our cities uninhabitable? Will we go on accepting enormous military spending?

But also: Will we still look suspiciously at other people who step close to us? Will we be able again to passionately kiss a person whom we met just an hour before?

In this extreme laceration of the fabric of meaning, which we are presently enduring, a writing machine has been put in motion. An immense schismogenetic poem is being composed. The intention of this poem is to produce the harmonic form of the mutation: absorbing the viral *ritournelle* that provokes mutation, and concatenating that *ritournelle* with the *ritournelles* of individuals, small groups, large crowds, social bodies, all collaborating to rewrite the poetical and computing software of social interaction.

Because writing is, ultimately, the main cosmo-poetic activity: the energy that allows us to go beyond the threshold.

Beyond the Breakdown

All of a sudden, what we have been thinking over the last fifty years has to be rethought from scratch. Thank God (is God a virus?) we have an abundance of extra time now that the old business is out of business.

I'm going to talk about three distinct subjects. One: the end of human history, which is clearly unfolding before our eyes. Two: the ongoing disintegration of the neoliberal model and the imminent danger of the techno-totalitarian rearrangement of capitalism. Three: the return of death to the scene of philosophical discourse, after its long denial by modernity.

Critters

Donna Haraway is the philosopher who best anticipated the ongoing viral apocalypse.

In *Staying with the Trouble* (2016), Haraway suggests that the agent of evolution is no longer Man, the conscious subject of history. History is losing ground as the chaotic complexity of events reduces and finally cancels the scope of the potency and effectiveness of conscious will.

Over the last decades, History has been slowly replaced by Her-story – and this replacement has accelerated with the pandemic, when the impotence of will has emerged most clearly.

We could call Her-story the evolution of the conjunctive interweaving between subvoluntary units, molecular entities, schismogenetic organisms, viruses that give birth to consciousness devoid of identity.

In this chaotic process, the centrality and (relative) sovereignty of the human, and particularly of human will, is lost.

Should we grieve over this loss of centrality, like the modern humanist nostalgics do? Yes, and no. Obviously our humanist sensibility – deeply rooted in our intellectual formation – suffers with this loss. And, obviously, the feeling of political impotence will fuel sentiments of rage and despair.

However, our intellectual imagination has to overflow the humanist imprint. We have to assume the form of the mutation, to rethink and to reimagine from the standpoint of a mutated relation between consciousness and evolution.

We should not seek comfort in the delusions of a techno-fix, as suggested by the contemporary transhumanist techno-maniacs, but we should look for a rhythm of life that re-creates the conditions for happiness in a mutated environment.

Human history is over, and the new agents of history are the 'critters', in Haraway's parlance. The word *critter* refers to small creatures who do strange things, like provoking mutations.

Burroughs speaks of viruses as agents of biological, cultural, linguistic mutation.

Critters do not exist as individuals. They spread collectively, as a process of proliferation.

The year 2020 should be seen as the year when human history started to dissolve – not because human beings have disappeared from planet Earth, but because planet Earth, tired of their arrogance, launched a micro-campaign to destroy their *Wille zur Macht*.

The Earth is rebelling against the world, and its agents are floods, fires and most of all critters, material critters (virus) and immaterial critters (poetry).

The agent of Evolution is no longer the conscious, aggressive and strong-willed human being – but molecular matter, micro-flows of uncontrollable critters who invade the space of production, and the space of discourse, replacing History with Her-story: teleological Reason is replaced by Sensibility and by a process of harmonisation with the sensuous chaotic becoming.

Humanism was based on the ontological freedom that the philosophers of the early Renaissance identified with the absence of theological determinism. Theological determinism is over, but the virus has taken the place of the teleological God.

The conscious teleology of politics is replaced by multiple strategies of contagious proliferation. Proliferation, the spread of molecular processes, replaces the macro-project called History.

Thought, art and politics are no longer to be seen as projects of totalisation (*Totalisierung*, in Hegel's sense) but as processes of proliferation without totality, as tools for the harmonisation of the body and of the soul with the chaotic becoming of the micro-macro-apocalypse.

Usefulness

After forty years of neoliberal acceleration, the race of financial capitalism has suddenly ground to a halt. Months of global lockdown, a long interruption of the production process and of the global circulation of people and goods, the tragedy of the pandemic ... all of this is going to break capitalist dynamics in an irreversible way. The powers that manage global capital at the political and financial level are desperately trying to save the economy, injecting enormous amounts of money into it. Billions, trillions ... figures that increasingly mean: zero.

All of a sudden money means very little.

Why give money to a dead body? Is it possible to revive the body of the global economy by injecting money into it? It isn't. Both the supply side and the demand side are becoming immune to the money stimulus, because this slump is not happening for financial reasons (like in 2008) but because of the body's collapse – and bodies have nothing to do with finance.

We are passing the threshold that leads beyond the cycle of labor–money–consumption.

When, one day, the body comes out from the confinement of quarantine, the problem will no longer be how to rebalance the relation between time, work and money or how to rebalance debt and repayment. The European Union was almost destroyed by its obsession with debt and balance and by its compulsion to coerce people into repaying their (metaphysical) debt. The result was that, during the pandemic, hospitals rapidly ran out of ventilators, doctors were overwhelmed by fatigue, anxiety and fear, and hundreds of thousands of people died.

This situation cannot be fixed by money, because money is not the problem. The problem is: What are our concrete needs? What is useful for life, for collectivity, for therapy?

In Spring 2020, money could not buy the protective masks that were not available. It could not expand intensive care departments that were long ago destroyed by the neoliberal reform of Europe's healthcare system and could not provide the vaccines that had not yet been developed.

Then the vaccines were developed, but they could not be produced in sufficient quantities because of the proprietary rule of corporate licences.

So, money is losing its charm and its power. Only social solidarity and scientific intelligence are alive, and they can become politically powerful. This is why I think that at the end of the global quarantine we won't go back to normal. Normal will never come back. What will happen in the aftermath has not yet been determined, and thus it is not predictable.

We face two political alternatives: either a techno-totalitarian system will relaunch the capitalist economy by means of violence and hyperexploitation; or human activity will emancipate us from the abstractions of capital, and a molecular society based on usefulness and equality will emerge.

The proliferation of a chaotic concretion of matter (the virus) has shattered any control that the capitalist abstraction had on the world, while, simultaneously, a global automaton is tightening the grip of its network of digital techno-control.

The Chinese government is already experimenting on a massive scale with techno-totalitarian capitalism. The techno-totalitarian reshaping of social life, anticipated by the provisional abolition of individual freedom for sanitary issues, may become the dominant trend of the time to come, as Giorgio Agamben has rightly pointed out in his recent controversial texts.[1]

Agamben offers a description of the present emergency and of the probable future. But we should go beyond the description of what is probable, moving instead towards what is possible. And the possible is contained in the breakdown of abstraction, in the dramatic return of the concrete body as a bearer of concrete needs.

Use value, long expelled from the field of economics, is back. Usefulness, long forgotten and denied by the capitalist process of abstract valorisation, is now the king of the social field.

The sky was clear in the days of the lockdown. The atmosphere was less polluted as cars could not circulate. Will we go back to the polluting, extractive economy? Will we go back to the normal frenzy of destruction for accumulation and of useless acceleration for the sake of exchange value? Quite certainly yes, we will go back to the poetics of economic growth at all costs. But it will not work. Chaos will prevail.

We will be forced to renounce any wish to return to an impossible normality: we will be forced to think of the creation of a society based on the production of the useful.

What do we need now? Now, in this immediate now, we need a vaccine against the malady, we need protective masks, and we need intensive-care equipment. And in the long run we need food, we need affection, and we need pleasure. And a new culture of tenderness, solidarity, and frugality.

What is left of capitalist power will try to impose a techno-totalitarian system of control over society. But the alternative will also emerge: a society free from the compulsions of accu-mulation and economic growth, a social life based on frugality and equality.

Pleasure

The third point I would like to reflect on is the return of mor-tality as the defining feature of human life. Capitalism has been a fantastic attempt to overcome death. Accumulation is the *Ersatz* that replaces death with the abstraction of value, the artificial continuity of life in the marketplace.

The shift from industrial production to info-work, the shift from conjunction to connection in the sphere of communica-tion, is the end point of the race towards abstraction, the main thread of capitalist evolution.

During a pandemic, conjunction is forbidden – stay at home, don't visit friends, keep your distance, don't touch anybody. An enormous expansion of time spent online is underway, unavoidably, while all social relations – work, production, education – have been displaced into this sphere that prohib-its conjunction. Offline social exchange is no longer possible. What will happen after months of this?

Maybe, as Agamben predicts, we'll enter the totalitarian hell of an all-connected lifestyle. But a different scenario is also possible.

What if the overload of connections breaks the spell? When the pandemic finally dissipates (assuming that it will), it's possible that a new psychological identification will have already been established: 'online' equals 'sickness'. The massive talk of death, the resonance of death in the pandemic imagination, may provoke a depressive effect on the psychosphere – or quite the opposite, it may reactivate our sense of time as enjoyment rather than as the economic postponement of joy.

At the end of the pandemic, at the end of the long period of isolation, people may simply continue to sink into the eternal nothingness of virtual connection, of distancing and techno-totalitarian integration. This is probable. But we should not be confined to the probable. We should discover the possibility that is hidden in the present.

After months of constant online connectivity, people might come out of their houses and apartments looking for conjunctions. A movement of solidarity and tenderness can arise, leading people towards an emancipation from connective dictatorship. We have to imagine and to create this movement of caressing, a reinvention of eros in the age of mandatory distancing.

Death is back at the centre of the landscape: that long-denied mortality, which makes humans alive.

3

Semiotics of the Virus

The viral storm defies political power and social potency, and a chaotic flow of possibilities is entering into the scape of evolution.

The social standards of the past have grown inept to measure, to estimate, to compare things: the priorities established by economic sciences are out of service, and they cannot grasp the becoming of social life shaken by the proliferation of the virus.

The cardinal dogmas of the political imaginary have lost their assertiveness, and we witness the impotence of politics to govern the chaotic events of the subvisible world. The faculty of will, the protagonist of the modern political scene, is blurred, unable to distinguish and to react.

For a few centuries, humans chose to forget their limits, and to fall for the delusions of political omnipotence and of scientific omniscience.

Now it's crystal clear: the complexity of Nature is far beyond the reach of our understanding, and the chaotic features of the world are far beyond our ability to govern them.

Those who pretend to be in control look ludicrous or pathetic, while the aggressive wolves who used to champion national pride and ethnic superiority are roaming around without knowing what to do, and their howling sounds shrill.

Economists, entrepreneurs and financiers pronounce monetary figures like magicians in old times pronounced spells. They pretend to tame the mounting wave of panic and depression by throwing money into the cabalistic sphere of financial abstraction. But their astronomical figures have failed to prevent the dissemination of the pandemic, and they will prove unable to prompt recovery.

As an effect of the long-lasting lockdown, millions of workers are losing their jobs. How long can the past balance of labour, salary and market be managed by public spending?

For the first time, the asymmetrical relation between economy and life is fully exposed. Monetary abstraction is running on empty. The world that emerges from the viral mutation wants to be interpreted and organised through new concepts, and social activity has to be reframed outside of the framework of salaried labour.

The history of modernity has been structured by the semiotic code of Economics: events, acts, and relations. In that framework semiotised by the register of the Economic code, time was priced and mathematically measured as the source of value.

Throughout the modern age, mathematics has expanded its sphere of relevance and functionality. The accumulation of financial capital was based on the final reduction of everything to mathematical operations.

Other registers were open, other codes were filtering experience: the mythological register (expressed by politics, ideology and religion) and the psycho-affective register (eroticism, friendship, desire, the Unconscious) were acting in the social psycho-sphere. But the main narrative thread of capitalism, the Hyper-Code (the semiotiser of all semiotisers), as it were, has been the increasing subsumption of every fragment of reality and of experience by the domain of abstraction, and finally the unchallengeable command of the economic code on the overall machine of human life.

Occasionally, the mythological code infiltrated the economic space, trying to impose different priorities: equality, happiness, peace, nation, identity. Revolutions have shaken the order of social reproduction, and they have tried with some success to insert ideological or religious principles in the ordinary business of life. Ultimately, though, the economic code regained the upper hand.

'There is no alternative,' said the economic master of the game.

Inside the semiotic dimension of Expansion (as long as expansion was set as the horizon of human action), the Economic principle was perfectly suited to function as the universal mode of coding human endeavours. Expansion meant Growth, and Accumulation.

The concept of growth, within the economic framework, does not refer to the amount of welfare, of useful goods and of pleasure that can be experienced, but to the abstract codification in monetary terms of the mass of products and services. So the accumulation of abstract value results from the exploitation of human time, transformed into abstract labour.

But the horizon of expansion has faded and now is disappearing.

The exhaustion of physical resources and the exhaustion of our nervous energies have led to the end of expansion. Stagnation looms, and the obsessive pursuit of plus-value has turned into destruction, production of the useless, production of destructive tools, and active production of malady and death.

We have been warned of the impending end of expandability since the year 1972, when *The Limits to Growth* was published. Since then capital expansion has come to depend less and less on the production of useful things and useful services and more and more on the destruction of physical resources of the planet, of the nervous resources of labourers, and of the quality of life, of air, of water.

As the semiotic horizon of Expansion faded and finally swallowed itself, at that point we have entered the semiotic horizon of Extinction. The year 2020 is the turning point.

After the smoke choking New Delhi in November and the Australian fires of December, we have gone through an all-encompassing mutation triggered by the proliferation of a virus: this subvisible material concretion has blocked the abstract machine of valorisation and accumulation.

The semiotic code of the Economy that in the past was dedicated to establishing priorities and measures is now replaced by a new semiotic code: Bios.

The biosphere is traversed by an agent that cannot be reduced to the abstract code of the Economy, and the virus is acting as a Universal Re-Codifier.

The system of economic priorities has imploded, unable to continue interpreting and coding Real Life.

Real life is now this: burning forests, melting ices, air pollution, pandemics. Therefore real life is replaced by digital networking, and bodily conjunction is replaced by machine connection.

Viral recoding and digital recoding run parallel in the cultural evolution of our time. In an article published in a Uruguayan online magazine, Gabriel Eira and Nicolás Guigou describe a viral pandemic in the context of the techno-cultural shift from analogical to digital capitalism. Viral proliferation, organic chaos and techno-linguistic automation are linked in their description in a very interesting way:

> Viruses are but algorithms of information (DNA and RNA) stored in proteins. Like in living organisms the virus's information evolves and reproduces, but it needs a hosting organism. The information contained in the virus has the ability to reprogram the extracted information so that the membrane of cellular identity explodes. Every reprogramming brings about dangers of data alteration, and this is helping the virus to mutate.[1]

According to Eira and Guigou, the analogical membrane of the twentieth century has been exploded by the concatenation of two mutational flows: one is the digitisation of social language, and the second is the epidemic spreading of the virus that is acting on three different levels of society. First, the immunitarian level that is reprogrammed by the physical contact with the virus. Second, the economic level that has been blocked, slowed, and finally jeopardised. And finally, the psychological level that is affected and traversed by conflicting impulses and by a dramatic change in expectations.

The invisible hand of the market has been reshaped by this double irruption.

The digital net has accelerated market dynamics during the last three decades; then the pandemic has blocked that acceleration.

The lockdown generates an effect of coalescence in which particles, tendencies and opposing forces agglutinate in an alchemic composition that is giving birth to the homunculus of twenty-first-century capitalism. This homunculus is not human and not individual; obedient to the overcoming of the analogical past, the homunculus is training during the time of confinement. The homunculus is not looking at the screen; he is penetrating in it and obediently receives in his body and skin the new and the old connections. In this digital capitalism the invisible hand of Adam Smith plays with the keyboard and the smartphone small screen ... Those unable to smoothly enter in the communicational matrix, those unable to comply with the digital work transformation, will be superfluous.[2]

The scenario described by Eira and Guigou – a progressive submission of the human to the automaton – is quite realistic, but not exhaustive, in my opinion.

We cannot be sure that the subjective disturbance will smoothly be reabsorbed and the economic cycle will slowly go back to normal.

The history of capitalism was the history of expanding domination of the abstract on the useful, but now the race towards abstraction has been intersected and broken by the abrupt insertion of a material proliferating concretion: the virus.

Since then bios has broken the chain of techno-linguistic automatisms and is now revealing the horizon of extinction. The prospect of extinction is going to recode all the events, the acts and the signs of the social sphere.

On one side it is possible to speak of the recoding described by Eira and Guigou: the digital recoding of life in all its forms. But on the other side we must speak of a biological and psychic recoding that intersects with and complicates the frame.

The task of philosophy now is to imagine a way to coevolute with the bio-semio virus: how to coevolute with the psycho-semiotic effects that the bio recoding of the world is going to enable.

Can we happily live with the universal recoding that is irreversibly underway? This is the aesthetic and ethical question that lies ahead.

4

The Spectrum and the Horizon

I was eighteen years old in 1968.

That year I began my first year of university, as a student of philosophy. I took part in the movement, I spoke in meetings, I was talking with friends all the time about what was happening in the world: Vietnam, the worldwide students' uprising, Black riots in the US, the cultural debates about neocapitalism and so on ...

I was not illiterate or uninformed.

Nevertheless, I do not remember discussing with my colleagues a subject that I only recently heard about: the pandemic flu that broke out in July of 1968. Generally speaking I have a good memory, but I cannot recollect anything about the H_3N_2 virus, also known as the Hong Kong flu.

It was not a minor accident in the history of viral outbreaks: it is considered to be the third most lethal pandemic in the twentieth century, after the Spanish flu of 1918–1919, and the HIV breakout of the 1980s.

The 1968 flu pandemic resulted in an estimated 1 million to 4 million deaths.

As many as 4 million fatalities, and I knew nothing about it until 2020. The Hong Kong flu was not part of the daily talk of the people (students, journalists, union workers, leftist intellectuals) that I met.

The first recorded instance of the outbreak appeared on 13 July 1968 in Hong Kong. By the end of July, extensive outbreaks were reported in Vietnam and Singapore.

By September 1968, the flu had reached India, the Philippines, northern Australia and Europe. The same month, the virus entered California and was carried by troops returning from the Vietnam War, but it did not become widespread in the United States until December. It reached Japan, Africa and South America by 1969.

More than a hundred thousand people died in the US.

And I was not aware of the flu.

Let's return to the year 2020. I've been talking about the coronavirus pandemic every day. Every conversation has revolved around this same subject, more or less.

Since February 2020, coronavirus has been the undisputed king of the mediascape. I think that poor Donald resents that the word *coronavirus* surpassed by far the name *Trump* in the mediasphere.

Numerous diaries of the lockdown have been published (one written by myself) and zillions of TV talk shows aired. The TV is showing scenes of people hospitalised, ambulances, doctors wearing masks.

Our life has changed in many ways: prolonged lockdowns, social distancing, a forced redesign of proxemics.

In February I was amazed by the news of the Wuhan lockdown, a city of 8 million inhabitants; then a few weeks later Italy locked down countrywide, and the lockdown lasted for two months.

The info-sphere has been saturated by the virus, and the info-virus has slowly penetrated the psycho-sphere and is saturating it.

Let's forget about the economic, technological and geopolitical effects of the pandemic. Let's focus on the mental dimension: the info-sphere and the psycho-sphere. What is happening in this dimension? What is going to happen next?

Why has our attention been so thoroughly catalysed by the bio-virus that immediately turned into an info-virus and is now turning into a psycho-virus?

Why have we reacted in a way that is so different from the way we reacted in 1968?

I know the Hong Kong flu pandemic spread in an era even before mass tourism and mass flight mobility, so people were not carrying pathogens with them in their travels and commercial exchanges, as is the case nowadays. The main difference in social perception of these pandemics probably lies in globalisation. In 1968 the circulation of people and goods was enormously less intense and rapid than now.

That's an answer to the question, but for me it's not enough.

I want to understand more about the different social perceptions of the two not-so-different outbreaks.

I know that here I'm striking a chord that is delicate and politically ambiguous, and I don't want to be misunderstood. My intention is not to question the sanitary policy that has been enforced in many parts of the world in order to contain the virus's spread and to slow down its rhythm.

I'm far from joining the right-wing negationists who want to reclaim the freedom to not wear a mask and to force people to work in crowded, dangerous factories despite the national lockdown.

That's not my point.

I'll try to define my point with a tentative concept: a Spectrum of Emotional Attention (SEA), which could also be called an Imaginary Spectrum.

Our imagination feeds within this spectrum, and it depends on the imaginary stuff that we receive from the surrounding info-sphere.

Our attention is attracted by the events that make sense in relation to what's relevant in the spectrum.

So I ask myself: What is the imaginary stuff that is saturating our spectrum nowadays? What is the difference between the present SEA and the SEA of 1968?

The contemporary SEA is depressed and overwhelmed by

flows of dark expectations, so we tend to react to those events that tend to confirm what we expect: extinction.

For years we have been half expecting the big event, and we identified the big event with the Covid contagion. Actually, the contagion has not been the cause of the breakdown. It has been the catalyst. Years of precariousness, impoverishment and humiliation have prepared the ground for the menial breakdown that the pandemic is catalysing now.

As the space for imagination has been crushed by the flows of the mediated imaginary, the space of mental autonomy has grown so narrow that we can barely choose what to think about, what to talk about, what to fantasise about.

Autonomy is not based on hating the enemy but on loving your own life, on liking the singularity that you are. How much do we love our lives nowadays? The continuous info-neural stimulation of the psycho-sphere has saturated attention, but the conscious organism that you are is perceiving itself on the basis of info-stimulation, not of self-perception. Joy is escaping because we are caught in a swirl of permanent excitement.

The future imagination is so dependent on the imaginary that is irradiated by the media-sphere that the collective unconscious was prepared for the implosion.

After the convulsive rebellions of autumn 2019, when the planetary body seemed to be exploding from Santiago to Hong Kong to Barcelona to Quito, the sentiment of a universal *no way out* pushed the collective mind to expect the blackout as the only way out.

Our nervous antennae are tuning in to the SEA, and they only detect depressive flows as the field of desire is invaded by them.

We are trapped in a sort of double bind: either we renounce the pleasure of feeling the fleshy tenderness of the other's body or we turn into potential bearers of malady, and possibly of death.

Is altruism leading to selfish isolation?

Are we led to undermine the very dynamics of empathy in order to ethically behave?

What is the psychological trace of social distancing in the long run?

How long will we be obliged to be cautious?

Can sensuousness coexist with caution, or is caution destined to jeopardise sensuousness?

I have no answers to these tremendous questions.

What I know is this: In this horizon that has been long hidden from view and is now being revealed by the viral apocalypse, two questions need answers.

The first is: Is it possible to dispel the perspective of extinction when subjectivation is shadowed by depression and autistic inclinations?

The second is even harder: Is a happy thought in the horizon of extinction possible?

That is not a purely philosophical question. It is existential, and political.

'Is a happy life possible in the horizon of extinction?' is the interrogation that every human being has to consider, as extinction is a certainty of individual existence. But now that interrogation is not to be considered in relation to the individual, but rather to humankind in its totality.

The Horizon after Protagoras

Modern humanism has followed the Protagoras principle:

> Man is the measure of all things – of all the things that are, that they are; of all the things that are not, that they are not.[1]

Humanism transformed that principle into a methodology for action, and according to that principle, politics emerged as the art of consciously governing things and events unfolding in historical time: the visible and knowable and therefore what was governable by human will.

Well, the Protagoras principle does not work anymore; we have exited the sphere of measurability. Man is no longer the measure of things, as things do not dwell anymore in the space of measurability.

What phenomena are we supposed to face, right now? Not the force of a human actor, not the method of political decision, but the proliferation of subvisible agents that cannot be reduced to exhaustive knowledge, and the multiplication of natural events like global warming, that enable irreversible dynamics on which the political has no grasp.

The tools of political reason are irrelevant at this level of smallness and of greatness. It's ridiculous to squabble about different forms of governability, as these forms cannot change the evolutionary drive that has been unleashed.

It does not matter anymore if the bus driver is sober or drunk when the bus has already veered off the highway and is plummeting down a five-hundred-meter ravine. Before crashing out of the highway it would have been better if the bus driver hadn't been drunk, but as we are now in free fall, it is not that important.

As we fall, the most current urgent problem is a subvisible particle whose intentions we are unable to guess, provided that the virus has intentions (and I think it does). The other urgent problem is the constant warming of the atmosphere, produced by factors that began to act in the past and are not ceasing to act.

Excessively small and extraordinarily large actors have invaded Protagoras's laboratory, and it has exploded. The method of politics is useless. Our will is unable to engender a reversal as these phenomena tend to feed on themselves and become irreversible.

Voluntary action seems only to amplify the processes of devastation: the probability of a war approaches when politics is impotent. Nationalism is the psychotic reaction to the impotence of will: as coasts are invaded by sea and forests burned by fire, masses of destitute people are nomadically migrating from one territory to another. Subsequently, territorialised people defend their territory where fires have not yet arrived.

Panic is the form that the will takes when will is impotent: the final stampede.

I think we should consciously assume extinction as the horizon of our time.

Keep calm, there is no escape, so stop frantically groping for a way out. Let's think how to spend this time that is distancing us from extinction.

Fear of death is a mistake of evolution, says Carlo Rovelli in *The Order of Time*. He explains that animals have an instinctive reaction of terror and flight when a predator approaches. It is a healthy reaction, because the fear of death saves them from an imminent threat. But we – apes with hypertrophic frontal lobes – have the ability to foresee the future, so we know death is our destiny, and we tend to stay alert all the time. Which is stressful and depressing. Everything has a limited duration, and the human race is no exception, concludes Rovelli.[2]

If we assume that extinction is the horizon of our time (which does not mean that extinction is unavoidable in an absolute sense but rather that, inside the apparently insurmountable conditions of capitalism, it is the most likely prospect), then the coordinates of our ethical political and affective expectations will change. First, we'll come to consider procreation as the most irresponsible action. Not only because procreation makes the final catastrophe more likely (Malthus is being discussed again, in a very different frame) but also for a much more personal and practical consideration: the possibilities for a happy life are rapidly shrinking to zero.

5

Psycho-Systemic Collapse

We must practise 'riding on the dynamic of disaster'.[1]

That phrase is a good description of our mental condition during the current earthquake, which is also a heart-quake, and a mind-quake.

The disaster is underway: it's impossible to avoid it, and it moves along a fault, a break line that is splitting the ground under our feet. We are forced to run along the line and try to avoid falling in the crevasse.

The question is, how to deal with the succession of catastrophic events that are awaiting around the corner in the wake of the twin apocalypses: the pandemic and the resulting lockdown and slowdown.

Some think that all we have to do is accelerate along the current path, leaving behind our belongings and our expectations: at a certain point everything will finally crumble and a new landscape of possibilities will emerge, as technology will generate a new rule, a new system. Those who think this way can be designated as accelerationists.

Others conclude, on the contrary, that we should restore some order, some symmetry in our environment and try to avoid the consequences of the disaster, overcoming the frailty of a generation growing within the condition of the absence of the father, that means the reduction of the symbolic force of the law, a loosened internalisation of the limit. As the flow of information and therefore accelerated time are fleeing too fast, the law has grown unable to govern, because government is based on rational processing – which takes time. The place of the father is empty, and these neopaternalists consider the solution to be a restoration of the paternal role under the warrant of a psychic order based upon the respect of law.

Both these stances – the accelerationist and the neopaternalist – miss the point both at the political and at the therapeutical level.

During the transmillennial decades, we were unable to consciously perceive the present, as we were ceaselessly compressed within the vertiginous flows of nervous stimulations. Then the virus slowed down the rhythm, and the horizon turned crepuscular, melancholic, hopeless.

Time is suspended and we don't know what will happen next. A return to the old normalcy? A comeback of the infection? Death?

A famous slogan of 1968: *Cours, camarade, le vieux monde est derrière toi* (Run, comrade, the old world is behind you).

But the years that followed '68 told a different story, because capitalism started running faster than the *camarade*.

The catastrophic experience that we are going through now is the point at which all that was possible becomes impossible, and what was considered impossible may become possible (or may not).

Don't forget that the etymology of the word *catastrophe* (*kata* = beyond, *strophein* = move) means a displacement beyond the visibility limit of the present, the disclosure of a possibility: what is possible is a configuration that does not belong to the jurisdiction of the impossible or to the jurisdiction of the necessary.

We must discover the possibilities that emerge from the internalisation of social distancing as the 'impossibility' of touching the other; then we must translate these possibilities in terms of social reconfiguration.

The Explosion of the Unconscious

Following neoliberal globalisation and the digital invasion of the info-sphere, the social Unconscious exploded.

If neurosis prevailed in Freudian discourse, the emergence of semiocapitalism mobilised nervous energies and forced hyperexpressivity.

Within the neurotic cycle of bourgeois society, desire was removed (repressed, sublimated and so on) in order to make room for the phantasmatic and an internalised potency of reality.

Then, in the psychotic cycle of semiocapitalism, what was removed was reality itself, in the name of unbounded potency of desire. But the potency of desire in not boundless, as it is submitted to the limits of the organism, to the limits of culture, of the economy and so on. The proliferation of lines of deterritorialisation accelerates stimulus beyond the breaking point: singular breathing becomes frantic, orgasmic joy becomes unattainable and panic overwhelms consciousness and body.

In a book published in 2010, *L'uomo senza inconscio*, Massimo Recalcati speaks of 'man without unconscious': in the post-modern age of hyper-expression our innermost dimensions have been pulled out by the acceleration of nervous stimuli and thrown into the chaotic open sprawl of the media imaginary.

What should we do in such a situation?

Recalcati answers: let's restore the authority of the father, the potency of reason, the law of the state.

But this answer is weak. The authority of the father, the potency of reason and the law of the state have crumbled because their rhythm was too slow in comparison with the mental pandemonium.

The info-nervous acceleration (deregulation plus globalisation plus digital network) provoked the explosion of the unconscious and the surfacing of the unconscious at the surface of social life.

In his time, Freud wanted to spread psychoanalysis like a plague within well-ordered repressive bourgeois society: he wanted to expose the abyss of the unconscious to a community that engaged in the repression of the drives of unchecked desire.

But info-nervous acceleration has eventually propelled and scattered all the psychic material that once upon a time was concealed. Psychotic hyperexpression has taken the place of neurotic compression.

For a long time it was clear that the world economy was entering a long-lasting stagnation. But capitalism started pushing society to run faster and faster, for the sake of the absolute dogma of growth, as the conceptual paradigm of capitalism is based upon expansion.

The report *Limits to Growth* pointed out the impossibility of unlimited growth in the year 1972. Recently Lawrence Summers, among other economists, speaks of secular stagnation. Nevertheless, it is hard to imagine a political way out from the stagnating economy of late capitalism, as the modern mind had been shaped by the expectations of growth, of expansion, of more things to consume. Nobody knew the way out from the stagnating and devastating labyrinth of capitalism. Now something has happened, pushing us out from the labyrinth. But where are we? What is life out of the labyrinth? We don't know.

Since the viral invasion and the ensuing lockdown, the scene has abruptly changed: the virus has paved the way to a subject-less revolution, a purely implosive revolution based on passivity and surrender.

'Just do nothing.'

All of a sudden this slogan takes a subversive sound: down with excitement, down with the useless anxiety that worsens the quality of life.

Literally: Nothing can be done anymore. So let's do nothing.

This is different from what happened in 2008, when the financial system was rescued by the intervention of the central banks and by the privatisation and destruction of social infrastructures as a way to rescue the bank system. This time, central banks and other financial institutions have no tools for relaunching the system.

So the global economy will not recover from the effects of this semio-psychotic virus, because economic science is unable to deal with sickness, panic, psychosis and fear. Therefore, capitalist economy seems to be short of solutions.

This time collapse did not come from financial or strictly economic factors: the crisis comes from the collapse of the body.

The social mind has unconsciously opted to slow down the rhythm, and the general demobilisation is a symptom of surrender: it is simultaneously an effect and a cause of the slowdown.

Biological functions have entered into passivity mode for reasons that have nothing to do with a conscious will or a political project. Tired of processing patterns that are more and more complex and of interpreting neuro-stimula that go faster and faster, humiliated by the impotence in front of the omnipotent techno-financial automaton, the nervous system has lowered the tension: this is a psycho-deflation.

All of a sudden the dynamics of disaster have changed their rhythm. Now we are dealing with a new problem that economics cannot solve: the problem of surviving in times of slowdown, and possibly of changing the rhythm of expectations so to frugally inhabit a slow environment and to turn stagnation into a new balance of need and satisfaction.

Economics is unable to deal with the pandemic, because this time the causes of the slump do not belong in the domain of the economy.

The stock exchange system has become the representation of a vanished reality: the supply and demand economies are unsettled and will be only marginally revived by money injected by the central banks. That means that the financial system is losing its grip: in the past, monetary fluctuations determined the amount of wealth that everyone could have access to. Now they no longer determine everything.

What society needs, now, seems to be beyond the reach of money.

...spension of the omnipotence of money may be the ...e to get out of the capitalist form and definitively ...the relation between social activity, money and access ...sources. A different conception of wealth seems to emerge ...m this disruption: wealth is not the amount of monetary equivalent I have, but the quality of life I can experience.

The economy is entering a recession, but this time the supply-support policies are not very useful; nor are the policies of support for demand. If people are afraid to go to work, if people are sick, or die, demand will not increase. If people are anguished as terror spreads, financial intervention will be no use. The rhythm of daily life has slowed, and people don't seem eager to go fast again.

Those who think that the machine can be reactivated thanks to the usual financial measures for recovery do not understand what is going on. They think that the problem is the relation between the financial market and daily business. But the problem is not the market; the problem is the soul. This time the slowdown has happened essentially in the biological and psychological dimension: it is the psycho-sphere that has suddenly come to a halt, and little by little it is trying to rewrite its internal rhythm.

Due to the decision to halt social activity flow and the economy flow, political leaders have certainly saved millions of lives during the Covid-19 pandemic.

But the April 2020 issue of the *Economist* – titled *A Grim Calculus* – observed that this will cost us a much higher number of lives in times to come. We are avoiding the massacre that the virus could cost us, but what scenarios do we prepare for the next few years, on a global scale, in terms of unemployment, production breakdown and distribution chains, in terms of debt and bankruptcies, impoverishment and despair?

The *Economist* editorial is reasonable, coherent, irrefutable, but only within the context of criteria and priorities that correspond to the economic form we call capitalism. An economic form that makes the allocation of resources, the distribution of goods dependent on participation in the accumulation of capital. In other words, it makes the concrete possibility of accessing useful goods dependent on the possession of abstract monetary securities.

Well, this model that has generated enormous resources for the construction of modern society has turned into a logical and practical trap that we have not found an exit from. But now, the way out has imposed itself automatically, unfortunately with violence. Not the violence of a political upheaval, but the violence of a virus. It's not the conscious decision of forces endowed with human will that have blocked the accumulation cycle, but the insertion of a heterogeneous corpuscle – like the wasp would be to the orchid – a corpuscle that began to proliferate until the collective organism was unable to understand and want, unable to produce, unable to continue.

This has stopped the reproduction of the cycle and sucked up huge sums of money that end up being of little or no use at all. We stopped consuming and producing, and for over a year we stayed home, looking at the blue sky from the window and wondering how all this will turn out. Bad, very bad, says the *Economist*, to whom the interruption of the cycle of growth and accumulation appears to be a catastrophic event that will lead to starvation, misery and violence.

I allow myself to disagree with the *Economist*'s catastrophic tone, because I intend the word *catastrophe* differently – as its etymology can also mean *a turning, beyond which you can see another panorama.*

So we have moved beyond the labyrinth; we have silently made that move that fifty years of loquacious struggles have failed to carry out.

The disruption has finally happened, but it has been a process without subjectivity.

Everything or almost everything stopped, and economic growth is not in sight. What is needed now is what has been lacking so far: a motionless subjectivity, the ability to passively change the course of social life, the ability to subtract social life from the accumulation principle, and to start a process aimed towards usefulness rather than growth, frugal equality rather than competition and inequality.

Will we be capable? I don't know, and above all I don't even know who that 'we' will be. Who will be capable of what?

No longer politics or the art of governance. Politics is incapable of any government, and above all it is incapable of any understanding.

The poor politicians seem to be haunted, staggering, anxious. The new game is the rhizomatic proliferation of ungovernable corpuscles. In this new game what is important is knowledge – not will.

Therefore, no longer politics, but knowledge. Yes, but what kind of knowledge?

Not the *Economist*'s knowledge, unable to leave the hall of mirrors of abstraction and valorisation, but knowledge of concrete usefulness, knowledge of the body, knowledge of the virus, knowledge of chemistry, physics, neurology and electronics: knowledge that does not translate into profit, but into usefulness and pleasure.

Do we need F-35 fighter aircrafts? No, we don't. They are useless. Those workers who now make a living producing weapons should be paid for doing nothing, which would be much more useful than doing what they are obliged to do at the present.

Do you know how many intensive-care units one could make out of a single F-35? Two hundred.

What if we decide to make people work only for the time necessary to produce what is useful? What if we give everyone an income regardless of their (otherwise useless) working time? What if we stop paying the debt, all the debts, every kind of debt, as the very word debt is now meaningless? What if we screw up international bonds that force us to pay huge sums of money to afford wars?

I have been thinking and writing these kinds of things for many years, but once upon a time these arguments were rantings of an extremist. No longer. These kinds of rantings will soon look like the only possible realism: there is no alternative.

I'm not hinting that the revolution of usefulness upon abstraction will happen soon and certainly. Not at all.

I say: This is necessary for the sake of humankind's survival. But if no subjectivity emerges, this revolution will not happen.

In an article titled 'Why the Global Debt of Poor Nations Must Be Canceled', published in the *New York Times* on 30 April 2020, prime minister of Ethiopia Abiy Ahmed explains with absolute clarity that fair and reciprocal treatment of others is necessary in a world of interdependence and interconnection (Ethiopia cannot both pay back debts and save lives during the pandemic). Only such a thing as a pandemic makes the thread that binds everyone visible. The evolutionary plan of the new (antimarket) rationality is that it now becomes 'convenient' (in a classic utilitarian sense) to collaborate and review the rules of the game. Among them, debt tyranny is the first to fall.

When I can't pay my debt to you anymore, my downfall is your downfall. The infection has made this clear. This concept is difficult for the German Protestant mind to accept since it views debt as a sin requiring atonement. But the depth of the economic breakdown will possibly oblige this prejudice to come to terms with the reality of necessary insolvency.

If we are not able to radically change the general form in which human activity takes place, if we are not able to get out of the model of debt, wages and valorisation, I would say that extinction is around the corner.

A third way between communism and extinction I do not see.

6

Freedom and Potency

People came to this country for either money or freedom. If you don't have money, you cling to your freedoms all the more angrily. Even if smoking kills you, even if you can't afford to feed your kids, even if your kids are getting shot down by maniacs with assault rifles. You may be poor, but the one thing nobody can take away from you is the freedom to fuck up your life whatever way you want to.

Jonathan Franzen, *Freedom*

To be entangled is not simply to be intertwined with another, as in the joining of separate entities, but to lack an independent, self-contained existence. Existence is not an individual affair. Individuals do not preexist their interactions; rather, individuals emerge through and as part of their entangled intra-relating.

Karen Barad, *Meeting the Universe Halfway*

Since the first days of the pandemic, and since the beginning of the ensuing lockdowns, public opinion has split between those who reject any limit to their personal freedom and those who support the regulation of social interaction.

The very borders between the political fronts, right-wing and left-wing, have been blurred on this point: the opposition to lockdown and sanitary regulation has been taken over by right-wing libertarians.

How can we explain the fact that the anarchists are respecting the rules, while the fascists are reclaiming their freedom to do what they like?

This reversal makes it clear that the political geography of the past century is out of service, but it is also revealing a philosophical misunderstanding that has traversed the history of modern politics. The concept of freedom, the unquestionable commonplace of the public discourse, has to be rethought, from the point of view of the present complexity, and the platitudes of the political talk have to be subjected to a critical investigation.

The squads of American supremacists who occupied with guns public places to protest anti-Covid restrictive measures were reclaiming their freedom and celebrated the Land of the Free.

What were they talking about?

Those people belong to a country that has written the word *freedom* in its founding papers but since the beginning omitted to mention the condition of slavery of millions.

In the first days of the Italian lockdown, in March 2020, when the political authorities decided to quarantine all the population (with the exception of those workers who were deemed indispensable), as the number of people testing positive was growing every day, some commentators, including the prominent philosopher Giorgio Agamben, rejected the rationale of the lockdown and the implied rules. This rejection was based on reasonable motivations: Agamben criticised the restrictive rules as 'techno-medical despotism', arguing that such rules were paving the way to a techno-authoritarian system of control. This consideration was not unfounded, I think: the wide intellectual aggression against Agamben that followed his statement seemed to me a symptom of conformism.

Nevertheless I did not join the ranks of the 'libertarians', and I did not share their critique of the lockdown measures, because I felt that their opposition was based on the manipulation of a concept that, even if superficially noble, does not sound philosophically well grounded and in the present conjuncture is sounding like an empty catchword: the concept of 'freedom'.

In a paradoxical turn of the tables, the fascists are claiming freedom against the leftist oppression. Some right-wing political criminals (Trump and Bolsonaro and their like) launched a campaign against restrictions, and the word *freedom* was the keyword of their authoritarian action.

Once upon a time romantic heroes died reclaiming freedom from tyrannical rule. Now the fascio-liberal heroes shout *freedom* and they mean *no sanitary masks*.

They are intimately persuaded that freedom is first of all the freedom of exploiting the work time of those who have the freedom only to be exploited or die. Within the sphere of economic inequality the word *freedom* only means entitlement, supremacy and violence. But now it is time to rethink the rhetoric of freedom and to disclose the conceptual aporias that this word contains.

The Rhetoric of Freedom Is Based upon a Misunderstanding

I'm questioning here the philosophical background of the rhetoric of freedom in the modern age and of the exploitation of this concept by the economic libertarians who have devastated social life in the last four decades and by the political libertarians who have used that kind of rhetoric to aggressively defend the white privilege and the Western domination of the world.

I do not pretend to fully develop this subject. I just want to outline the philosophical genesis of the false concept of freedom and of the pragmatic paradoxes that this fake produces in the real world.

The political abuse of the word *freedom* is based on a linguistic misunderstanding: three different levels of existence are confused, and three different meanings of this word are mixed, scrambled and identified so that the word can be used in such a way as to identify slavery as freedom: the most automatic and least free regime that ever existed on planet Earth in the last three thousand years (namely: neoliberalism, which is based on the absolute rule of capital accumulation, on massive slavery of labour and on automation of semiotic relations) is proposed as the symbol of freedom.

The systematic impoverishment of social life and depletion of the planet's resources are labelled 'free enterprise'. But the origin of manipulation is based on the ambiguousness of the concept of freedom, in its modern philosophical genealogy.

My first conceptual move will be to differentiate three different meanings of the concept: ontological, political and physical.

The modern concept of freedom arose in the humanistic perspective as ontological freedom. Free will is conceivable when humans are free from the divine determination.

In the framework of humanistic thought, the human adventure is not the implementation of the universal God's knowledge and providence but the practical deployment of individual and collective projects.

Even if God is the source of every entity existing in the world, even if God's knowledge contains the determination of every event occurring in the world, when God gave life to Adam, he also decided not to assign any necessary destiny to the human being.

According to the will of God, human action is not predetermined by his omnipotent will.

The human exception consists essentially in this: the possibility of choosing and acting according to free will; God wants us to be independent from his own resolutions.

This ontological freedom is the condition that made it possible to conceive the effectiveness of voluntary action, and this is the condition of history as conscious creation. The succession of time takes a historical feature when voluntary action becomes effective transformation of nature.

According to Niccolò Machiavelli, human will is endowed with the potency to freely rule over random ventures and events and therefore to submit to the capricious nature of Fortuna (that in Latin means the unpredictability of human events) to the intentions of power.

Potency and Freedom

Potency and free will are linked in the modern political imagination. The problem is that this link is misconceived: the rhetoric of freedom, in fact, assumes that the will is unbounded and that potency is inscribed in the space of freedom. This is wrong and misleading.

If we consider that action is happening in the reality of the physical world where physical forces are confronted, we are led to understand that freedom exists only in the space of potency.

We are free to do what we have the potency to do.

Only in the space of our potency are we free to choose and to act.

The Spinozian question 'What can a body do?' is the translation of the question 'What is the extent of its freedom?'

Voluntary action is not evolving in a space of infinite openness; the various dimensions of the real (the natural world, technology, the decay of the body and the presence of other bodies) act as entanglements of our will.

If we downplay the relation between limitations of the entangling context and potency of the subject of will then we are left with an empty freedom.

Disentangling our action from the tangles that precede the existence of the will itself: this is the core of what I prefer to call autonomy rather than freedom. In modern times, from

Machiavelli to Lenin, human will has managed to act in a rela-
tively autonomous way, because the potency of the entangling
context was not overwhelming: low density of technology,
slow circulation of information. In this context the political
will was effective in changing the relation between man and
nature, by submitting nature to the technique.

The potency of will has decreased in proportion to the
growing complexity and potency of the entangling *Umwelt*. So
in the late modern age the potency of will has been challenged
by the omnipotence of capital and eroded by the penetration
of economic and technical automatisms in the fabric of time.
At this point the mythology of freedom is reduced to a mere
trompe l'oeil, as we delude ourselves by believing that choice
is possible and that voluntary action can change the course of
events according to the will of the majority of citizens, while
the scope of political action is contained and entangled by
techno-linguistic automatisms resulting from the marriage of
capital and technology.

In the wake of the humanistic breakthrough, the concept
of freedom was shaped as a political concept: given the free
will of human beings, they decided to become citizens, so that
freedom could be the condition of the artificial order of social
life – freedom turned into independence from any established
power and took the form of democracy. Eventually, however,
techno-capitalism has emptied democracy of its potency,
exposing the fragility of freedom as a political concept.

The pandemic breakdown is exposing the impossibility of
freedom in the conditions of hypercomplexity that are produced by the spread of a virus in the physical body of society.

During recent times, science and politics managed to reduce
the complexity of the world to the regularity of physical laws
and to the intentionality of political laws. No more so: scientists have come to understand that physical laws are but an
uncertain approximation, not exhaustive of the complexity
of matter and time. And citizens have come to understand

that political decision is less and less relevant as the technical *Umwelt* is growing more complex and automated.

Science and politics have proved unable to exhaustively master the subliminal and the supraliminal of evolution: the biological and neurological microprocesses, the catastrophic planetary macroprocesses that capitalist extractivism has unchained.

As we are forced to acknowledge our impotence, our inability to freely choose the context in which we live, a sense of frustration is spreading and nurturing a cultural wave of rage, desperation and aggressiveness.

In *Die Antiquiertheit des Menschen* (1962), Günther Anders speaks of the sense of impotence that we feel as our technical knowledge has produced macroforces like the nuclear bomb. We are humiliated by the effects of our own cognitive potency, and this humiliation is fuelling the neoreactionary movements of our time: proud declarations of ignorance are aimed to restore the superstitions of identity.

Political free will was effective (to a limited extent) when our action was dealing with the action of other fellow humans and with the environment of the man-made city. But in late modern times we have been obliged to deal with the macroforces of nature revolting against anthropic subjugation and with the macroforces of automation (particularly of cognitive automation) that are escaping the will of its creators.

Simultaneously we are obliged to deal with the microforces of viral pervasion that are not only jeopardising our physical organisms but also the economic, semiotic and affective spheres.

Ironically the extent of our knowledge is reducing the extent of our freedom: macrotrends and microevents escape the grasp of political will and curtail the scope of human freedom.

Virus and Singularity

What is left of freedom and will when techno-capitalism has inscribed its priorities as an absolute necessity in every aspect of the social relation? What is left of free opinion when corporate media have saturated every instant of attention?

Political freedom has been undermined by the widening range of technical prescription, by the insertion of technical automatisms in language.

All of a sudden, however, something happened that was not predicted: the virus – the swift and unstoppable diffusion of a subvisible microentity whose mission is proliferation and whose occasional power is jeopardising the organism.

This biological agent has triggered a chain of sanitary transformations of daily life, and it is (not so) slowly provoking disruption in the economic, in the geopolitical and last but not least in the psychological domain.

The pandemic has broken the economic automatisms of supply and demand, of production and distribution, provoking a collapse of the capitalist economy and the disruption of the global machine. Simultaneously it is creating new automatisms, not less invasive than those inscribed in the economic machine: sanitary automatisms, techno-mediated distancing and psychological obsessions.

The proliferation of the virus acts as a purveyor of chaos: because of the chaos produced by a subvisible concretion of biological matter, conscious will loses its potency, so that politics is reduced to implementation of sanitary rules. These rules, however, are not based on deterministic certainty, because the circulation of the subvisible concretion of matter that we name *virus* is infinitely variating. Scientists have searched for some regularities in the contagion, so as to predict the evolution of pandemics and arrange means of protection and cure.

A second wave of the contagion followed in the second half of the year 2020. But as the months passed we realised the waves will not number one or two or three; they will be uncountable, like the sea waves. The virus did not begin one winter day in Wuhan; it has existed for ever, and only recently it mutated into something dangerous for the human body, and even if we prevent further spread (by the vaccine or other means), it is not going to disappear: it is going to evolve into something different that will be less dangerous, more dangerous, or not dangerous at all for the human organism.

In the physical world there is no end: matter is becoming, decomposing, recomposing, emerging and disappearing from sight. But only our consciousness is something that begins somewhere and that terminates at a certain point. Only consciousness has the ability to become nothing. All other things evolve.

Consciousness is the only thing in the universe that may conceive of nothingness and may evolve into nothingness.

The virus is not nothing, and it is not going to become nothing: it is going to evolve into something different.

Looking at the evolution of pandemics, we can note some regularity, but this is scarcely relevant from the point of view of the 'contagion' event, which happens in unpredictable ways. Even if some determinism is implied in the transmission of the malady, the contagion is continuously triggering unpredictable emergencies, because the rules of this determination escape the scope of our understanding and of our conscious will.

On one hand the virus is continuously changing its nature and intensity; on the other, the endangered organism is a singularity that does not correspond to a homogeneous model, and it is continuously mutating in the context of environmental, technical, economic, sexual conditions in which it evolves.

The Quantum Leap of (Un)consciousness

If matter is evolving in a deterministic way, and knowing the exact position and relation of every particle of reality allows the knowledge of the future evolutions, why is it that we cannot predict the future configurations of the world?

Is it because the infinite complexity of the inner physical determinism cannot be processed by our limited potency of comprehension and prognostication?

Or is it because matter itself evolves in a nondeterministic way?

This dilemma, which runs through modern philosophy from Laplace determinism to quantic indetermination, takes on a crucial importance when we speak of the present relation between neuroscience and psychoanalysis and of the future evolution of the mind.

Does neurological matter act in a deterministic way on our psychological and cognitive behaviour, or is the relation between neurological brain and conscious mind essentially indeterministic?

What is the quantum leap that differentiates mental activity from neurological dynamics? What is the divergence between the physical dynamics of the brain and the emergence of thought?

The irruption of the virus in the landscape of the contemporary world, and particularly in the landscape of the unconscious intimate foreign land that Freud named the Unconsciousness, has revealed the fallacy and the emptiness of the pretension of freedom.

Interpreting the signs of the Unconscious and translating those signs into conscious choices is the pathway to freedom as the nondeterministic elaboration of the possibilities entangled in the determinism of physical and neurological matter.

We cannot be free, strictly speaking. We can gain autonomy

from some natural or social restriction. Autonomy depends on potency that we can deploy. Autonomy in fact means potency of imagination and of action.

As William James expressed it, 'My first act of free will shall be to believe in free will.'[1]

Here we can see the gap between neurosciences and psychoanalyses, between the physical determinism of neurology and the indeterminability of desire, even if this gap is absolutely singular in its genesis and manifestation and cannot be reduced to the scientific exactitude of determination.

Part II

The Imminent Psycho-sphere

7

Unconscious/*Verdrängung*

Unconscious and *Verdrängung*

Before Freud made the concept of the Unconscious the central pillar of psychoanalysis, the word had been used by Friedrich Schelling, the German philosopher who conceived of the relation between history and the Absolute in terms of sensibility, rather than of Reason. Schelling:

'The Absolute, for the sake of consciousness, separates itself into conscious and unconscious, the free and the intuitant.'[1]

Schelling contrasts the conscious to the unconscious in terms of an opposition between free consciousness and passive intuition, which is a sort of sensitive interpretation of the magmatic flow of surrounding reality.

Freud founds his vision of the unconscious in a different context: the activity of the mind beyond neurological reduction. Starting from contemporaneous research on neurological disturbances that led to neurotic behaviour, such as Jean-Martin Charcot's studies of hysteria, Freud aimed to disentangle the analysis of psychic suffering from the exclusive domain of neurology, focusing on the polarity between sexuality and language.

In order to overcome neurologists' reduction of mental activity and its pathological manifestations, Freud distinguished the conscious activity of the mind (or Ego) from the unconscious, which refers to the dynamics that precede the conscious enunciation and constantly interfere with it.

Furthermore, Freud distinguished the id (or German *Es*), which is based on natural instincts and drives, and the super-ego, which can be seen as an internalisation of the moral and social pressures that come from culture and from the surrounding environment.

This dynamic is not consciously governed by the individual, even if it deeply influences the discursive sphere. The basic task of psychoanalysis, at least according to Freud, is the interpretation of the hidden text of the unconscious that expresses itself in metaphorical ways, through involuntary mental associations, concealments and disruptions.

This work of interpretation is supposed to enable the disclosure of those mental contents that have been concealed to the conscious mind and have been enigmatically transformed by an act of *Verdrängung* (erroneously translated in English to *repression*, and better translated as *denial*).

In an effort to enable the coherence of a conscious self, *Verdrängung* acts on the contents of lived experience by denying access to consciousness. It acts on those contents of experience and of memory that might be dangerous for the psychological integrity of the self.

In *Civilization and Its Discontents*, Freud regards *Verdrängung* as an unwavering and constitutive trait of social relations:

> We cannot fail to be struck by the similarity between the process of civilisation and the libidinal development of the individual. Other instincts are induced to displace the conditions for their satisfaction, to lead them into other paths. In most cases this process coincides with that of the *sublimation* (of instinctual aims) ... It is impossible to overlook the extent to which civilisation is built up upon a renunciation of instinct, how much it presupposes precisely the non-satisfaction (by suppression, repression or some other means?) of powerful instincts. This frustration dominates the large field of social

relationships between human beings. As we already know, it is the cause of the hostility against which all civilisations have to struggle.[2]

Collective Unconscious

In the current context of viral mutation, I'm interested in revisiting the concept of the unconscious for reasons that are not strictly relatable to psychoanalytic theory. My focus here is the process of signification, and the faculty of imagination within it, as a means of enlightening the anthropological turn that is provoked by the pandemic.

Signification implies various levels of mental elaboration.

At the cognitive level, signification is based on the actions of structures of perception and of languages that are inscribed in the natural mind – but also in the evolution of the technical and relational environment.

Basic cognitive automatisms, deep mental structures wired in the brain, help us to interact with the environment. But these structures are not natural immutable forms, because they are evolving in the relation between mind and the environment.

The unconscious, as Deleuze and Guattari proclaim in *Anti-Oedipus*, far from being a mere depository of the denied contents of experience, is a force of production, actively emanating flows of dynamic and desire. The creative potency of the unconscious, in fact, consists in its ability to continuously reshape the inner structures of the mind.

The crucial idea of *Anti-Oedipus* is that the Unconscious is not a theatre but a factory.

The unconscious is a dynamic factor of conscious behaviour, not a receptacle of mental materials rejected by consciousness: it disturbs, disrupts and reshapes the conscious dimension, so that new configurations can emerge from a magmatic unconscious background.

For Ignacio Matte Blanco, the unconscious is a nondenumerable dimension, one resistant to the order of rationality:

'The unconscious deals with infinite sets that have not only the power of the denumerable but also that of the continuum.'³

The concept of continuum here gains relevance in opposition to the concept of the discrete: rational discourse is based on the combination of discrete units, while the unconscious acts as a magmatic continuum.

My concern with the concept of the unconscious, however, is not strictly psychoanalytic, as I said. What I want to understand is the social dimension of the mind, what I call the psycho-sphere (the sphere in which the flows of the imaginary circulate, interweaving so as to shape the imagination).

Can we speak of a collective unconscious?

From a strictly psychoanalytic view the unconscious is individual, but in a broader anthropological frame we can say that the individual workings of the unconscious are fed and transformed by the flows that proceed from the psycho-sphere, which is a collective dimension.

The psycho-sphere is not the aggregation of individual flows but the space in which information circulates (info-sphere), in the neurophysical form of nervous stimulation.

Notoriously, the concept of the collective unconscious was first proposed by Carl Gustav Jung, who wrote in 1943, 'In so far as we, thanks to our Unconscious, share the historical collective psyche, we spontaneously live in a mythological world of werewolves, of demons, of magicians and so on … because these things have been inhabiting the past ages as very intense affects.'⁴

In the wake of the modern enlightenment, scientific rationality has taken the place of mythological thought. Nevertheless, the legacy of the past has not disappeared: it stays in the common depository of the collective unconscious.

Therefore in Jung the collective unconscious can be defined as 'a sediment of experience, and simultaneously an *a priori* of experience itself, an *imago mundi*, shaped over eons.'⁵

But this is not my point: I'm not interested in the traces of past symbolisation, but in the present dynamics of the transformation of the mind in relation to the environment. I'm not interested in the legacy of mythological symbolism and its sedimentation in the collective unconscious, but in the current dynamics of the social mind; its premonitions, predispositions, its pathology and evolution.

I want to map the becoming of the psycho-sphere and the emergence of new mental configurations from this evolution. From the point of view of the present threshold we do not see a linear, deterministic thread of becoming, but we see a wide range of possible becomings. Not an emerging pathology, but a range of disturbances, interweavings, superpositions leading to possible unpredictable breakthroughs.

Beyond the pandemic threshold we should not expect unilateral transformations in the social mindset and in the deep modalities of cognitive elaboration. What we can do, now, while the pandemic is raging, is to map the mutation, describing the phenomenology of a trauma that is underway, so as to outline the possible (diverging and conflicting) outcomes, in terms of psychopathology and in terms of mental reshaping and the emergence of new psycho-scapes.

Unheimlich Everywhere

In *Das Unheimlich* (1919) Freud defines the psychological experience of something that is simultaneously familiar and strangely out of place: when a familiar event or a familiar object appears in an unsettling, eerie or taboo context, we are disturbed, ambiguously surprised or sometimes totally terrified. Unfamiliar, sinister, disquieting, uncanny are the possible definitions of this disarrangement of the daily experience and of the common environment.

In order to explain the concept of *Unheimlich*, Freud refers to the literary works of E. T. A. Hoffmann: unfamiliar details in quite familiar contexts, or the sudden appearance of something that we know very well in a context of painful chaos.

Furthermore, according to Freud, uncanny effects often result from instances of the repetition of the same thing, linking the concept of 'uncanny' to the concept of compulsive repetition. The feeling of uncanny may be seen as the sudden incongruous emergence of the unconscious in the familiar environment in which we live.

I would say that during the pandemic, the *Unheimlich* has come out of the margins and has invaded the whole life-scape: precautions, distancing, sanitary masks, every aspect of social interaction is proxemically redefined, and we are continuously inserting unfamiliar details into the daily routine.

Large parts of the population – all those who have not totally stopped their social interactions – are obliged to a constant thermometrisation of every aspect of life. Fever, cough, sneezing are possibly symptoms of a transformation of the social status – the sick are not only marginalised in the social activity but also have to be insulated, in order to deactivate the contagion. Looking for care implies self-reporting.

The spread of *Unheimlich* in the whole of life sediments a sort of estrangement of the living environment, a sort of recombination of the symbolic space.

Clearly the pandemic breakdown has acted and is acting as a trauma: a long-lasting low-intensity trauma, a slow-motion trauma being deployed through a period of time whose span we cannot at present predict.

From a cognitive point of view, a trauma can be viewed as a temporary disarrangement of the cognitive chain – first as a breakdown of the nervous automatisms that normally regulate chains of perception-reaction.

The coronavirus explosion has to be analysed at many different levels. Initially, it is a biological and medical crisis whose danger (lethality, physical and neurological consequences) can be valued in different ways: extremely high, or mild.

Some commentators think that the danger of the coronavirus has been overstated, as the lethality of the virus seems to be low, with the exception of very old people and people with pre-existing pathologies.

But I'm not speaking of the physical lethality of the virus here. I argue that the effect of the bio-virus is not socially limited to the physiological level.

In a few months of pandemic, the virus had infected the info-sphere, saturated daily talk, electronic media, and social networks, fuelling fear, panic and depression, and finally turned into a psycho-virus.

The catastrophic effects of the viral cycle are already visible in the economic sphere, provoking massive unemployment and a dramatic downturn of economic demand with depressive consequences in the long run.

Since the beginning of the outbreak and the following lockdown, countless psychologists worldwide have remarked on an increase in panic crises, depression and suicide, with a spread of depression both in the young, who are deprived of affective exchanges, and the old, who are exposed to contagion, hospitalisation and possibly death in isolation. But we must try to prefigure the possible evolution(s) of the psycho-sphere and the imminent psycho-scapes of the collective unconscious. How the human mind will adapt to the pandemic apocalypse is far from clear, but we can imagine that the trauma will enable psychological and even cognitive mutation. Will we be able to consciously elaborate this mutation, or will we be overwhelmed and totally disempowered?

The Psychotic Turn of the Psycho-Sphere in the Late Twentieth Century

The psychopathological regime described by Freud was centred on neurosis, which appears as 'the result of a struggle between self-preservation and the requests of libido, a struggle in which the Ego wins at the price of pain and renouncements'.[6]

In *Civilization and Its Discontents*, Freud asserts that modern civilisation is based on the necessary removal (denial or displacement) of the individual libido and on the sublimating organisation of the collective libido. Discontent is insurmountable within the frame of civilisation, and the goal of psychoanalytical therapy is to cure through language and anamnesis the neuroses it produces in us.

As long as the process of production was based on the mobilisation of physical energies, in the industrial age the expression of bodily desire was to be contained and repressed in order to invest energies in labour and accumulation. The repression of libido plays a fundamental role in the generation of neurosis: repressing sexual desire and the craving for freedom in many fields of life, particularly for women, was a precondition of the social order.

But the overall transformation of social life that was brought about by digital technology changed the psychological landscape in the late twentieth century in such a way that at a certain point the Freudian description was perceived as outdated, at least in terms of psychopathology.

Since the last decades of the last century, neurosis has faded as a dominant mental pathology, and a new set of psychological disturbances have emerged.

The neoliberal turn has marked a transformation of the info-sphere, increasing the intensity and velocity of the relation between info-sphere and psycho-sphere, and the effect of this change is this: repression is replaced by hyperexpression; denial is replaced by a sort of emergence of the unconscious flow on the visible scene.

Baudrillard denounced this excess of expressivity as the essential perturbation of the post-industrial regime of simulation and seduction, and this led him to criticise the Deleuze-Guattarian emphasis on desire.

The rhizomatic model outlined by Deleuze and Guattari has to be seen not only as a route map for a possible process of liberation but also and mostly as the account of a transformation in labour and capital and in the very process of signification.

As the rhizome theorised by the authors of *A Thousand Plateaus* has been implemented by neoliberal globalisation and the digital network, the signification process has been accelerated and complexified up to the point of exploding. The very relation between the unconscious sphere and conscious activity has been broken: the proliferating media flows have invaded the space of the unconscious and simultaneously allowed the unconscious to circulate everywhere, so that at the end of the twentieth century the neurotic landscape described by Freud is replaced by a psychotic explosion of flows of unconsciousness invading the space of political discourse, economy and mediascape.

The source of neurotic pathology is an act of concealment: subconscious contents are denied access to the visible space of rational consciousness, and this denial results in a sense of oppression and frustration. This is the core of neurosis in Freud's understanding.

Later on, however, the acceleration of the semio-sphere, and the following intensification of nervous stimulation, have exposed the contents of the unconscious pushing them into full light. Mind suffering at this point comes from an excess of light, not from the darkness of *Verdrängung* but from the compulsive excitement of desire rather than from concealment and denial.

An excess of visibility, the explosion of the info-sphere and an overload of info-neural stimuli: the exploding psychosis of the semiocapitalist age is rooted here.

Not repression, but hyperexpressivity is the background of the (post-Freudian) Second Unconscious: this is the source of the psychopathology that frames the neuro-sphere of the neoliberal age: attention deficit disorders, dyslexia and panic.

But now, when I write these pages, in the year 2020 that is marked by the coronavirus pandemic, something is changing in the magmatic sphere of the unconscious, up to the point that I dare to say that we are probably passing a threshold: we are stepping into a third age of the psycho-sphere, and therefore into a Third configuration of the Unconscious.

The Third Psycho-Sphere

During spring 2020 of the global lockdown I became slowly aware that a mutagenic wave was infiltrating the psycho-sphere, provoking a slow but durable change in proxemic perception, sexuality and sensibility at large.

In the synthetic recollection of the late modern evolution of the psycho-sphere that I've outlined above, I say that in the second part of the past century the borders between consciousness and unconsciousness shifted, revealing new dimensions of mental disease and passing from a neurotic regime to a psychotic regime of pathology.

Subsequently the hinges that once upon a time were holding together the universe of sensibility, of eroticism and affectivity began to crack. Now the trauma is affecting erotic sensibility and empathy as a whole but we cannot predict what kind of adaptation, what kind of reshaping, is going to succeed, because the trauma sets in motion ambiguous mutations: fear and new forms of expression of craving, avoidance, and phobic sensibilization to the body of the other.

We cannot fully describe the subjectivity that will emerge beyond the threshold of the psycho-deflation, because this is largely dependent on the cultural action of art, of poetry and of the psychoanalytical imagination.

Psychoanalytical interpretation must give way to schizo-analytical imagination. Only transcending the norms for interpretation forged by the mental experience of the past, we can help in shaping the evolution of the collective unconscious.

What will be the long-lasting effect of the viral invasion on the affective and sensuous perception of the outside world?

The trauma is not immediately evident. The trauma is working slowly, and first of all it has emerged as psycho-deflation, slowing down the rhythm of daily life and provoking a return of long-forgotten boredom.

Simultaneously, the trauma has fully mobilised the technology of distant communication, provoking the increasing dependence of the social mind on the screen, on digital hyper-stimulation without contact.

During the year 2020 we stayed on the threshold, in a state of calm punctuated by panic: a distanced relation with surroundings, the world reduced to an apartment, and the public sphere utterly virtualised.

However, in this ocean of calm and silence, we are witnessing a widespread increase in anxiety, numbness and depression. What can be found out beyond the threshold? What will we be able to create beyond the threshold? As the unconscious is not a theatre in which a prewritten play is performed, but a laboratory of cutting and pasting, a laboratory of dance, of syntonization with the rhythm of chaos, what sort of configurations will emerge in the collective unconscious?

We are just starting upon a drift, a path that is not already written in the map. We are entering an oscillation, a prolonged fluctuation between anguish and desire.

The imperative of the social superego may change its direction.

In the Freudian domain, the superegoic imperative demanded a renunciation of the *Trieb*, of the impulse to pleasure. In contrast, the neoliberal imperative directed towards sustaining and mobilising social craving was celebrating enjoyment and competitive aggressiveness. The restless pursuit of joy that was ceaselessly evaded, the frantic attempts to be a winner, always frustrated by reality.

What now?

The superego emerging during the pandemic is based on responsibility. But the problem is: What does responsibility mean? What are the stakes of being responsible?

Respecting the other by distancing?

Renouncing the pursuit of pleasure, and refusing pleasure to the other?

Avoiding desire, internalising culpability?

That would be a recipe for depressed and isolated psychological states, and in the long run a recipe for violence.

The intimate foreign land (*Innere Ausland*) of the unconscious exploded during the age of global connection and hyperexpressivity; then, in the wake of the viral collapse a sort of crepuscular silence followed, a fading of energy, and a game of reciprocal culpabilisation invaded the space of sociality.

How can we overcome panic and phobia?

I return to the 1980s for reflection, and I am reminded of the effects that acquired immunodeficiency syndrome provoked in the sexually transgressive landscape of the time: that disturbance, provoked by the retrovirus in the erotic imagination, put in motion a displacement of sexual energy that in the following decade paved the way to the pornographic scene of connective eroticism.

From an aesthetic and cultural point of view, AIDS inaugurated the transition towards the anthropology of virtualisation: connectivity separates desire from pleasure, establishing a cycle of excitement without conjunctive fulfillment.

However, that syndrome concerned only a marginal part of the social and erotic landscape: only the exchange of blood enabled infection.

Now it's different: the exchange of saliva, the proximity of bodies, the exposition to the breath of the other can have a pathogenic effect: a widespread phobic sensibilisation to the other's skin may be expected to infiltrate the collective unconscious, poisoning the sources of that con/spiration that makes life pleasurable.

We may outline a scenario of psycho-mutation towards an autistic regime of affective and social relations and an ensuing disturbance in the erotic imagination. Mutual bodily suspicion will be preceding and hindering mutual desire. A phobic sensibility is possibly going to be internalised.

Furthermore, a xenopathic reaction of the skin would open the door to depression and aggressiveness.

Sympoetic Critters

A new empty space is opened to the psychoanalytic imagination and concomitantly to poetic creation.

What kind of tools do we have for a therapeutic elaboration of this new configuration of the psycho-sphere?

During a Zoom seminar with a class at Hunter College organised by my friend Daniel Bozhkov, a participant whose name is Chen said something interesting: 'Poetry is the critters of language'.

Critters, in Haraway's parlance, are small entities, subvisible creatures that proliferate everywhere and transform the composition of the living world, enabling mutation.

Chen's suggestion is enlightening: the structured building of language is crumbling, eroded by the infiltration of an unspeakable bio-info matter in the psycho-sphere. At this point, poetry consists in the emanation of linguistic particles for dissolution and recomposition. Haraway: 'We must somehow make the relay, inherit the trouble, and reinvent the conditions for multispecies flourishing, not just in a time of ceaseless human wars and genocides, but in a time of human-propelled mass extinctions and multispecies genocides that sweep people and critters into the vortex. We must "dare 'to make' the relay; that is to create, to fabulate, in order not to despair."'[7]

Transmigrant critters enable an inter-species relation that may go beyond the limits of the human.

Perhaps as sensual molecular curiosity and definitely as insatiable hunger, irresistible attraction toward enfolding each other is the vital motor of living and dying on earth. Critters interpenetrate one another, loop around and through one another, eat each another, get indigestion, and partially digest and partially assimilate one another, and thereby establish sympoietic arrangements that are otherwise known as cells, organisms, and ecological assemblages.[8]

The virus is an example of what *critter* means: a principle of a-signifying symbiotic and sympoetic creation.

The virus is a-signifying: it is not intended to bear a meaning, it is not a sign, but it is a micro-material corpuscle that bears in-itself information, something that gives unintended form to the organism, while pursuing (intended) proliferation. The information inscribed in the virus acts on the organism, jeopardises the immune system of the organism, but also jeopardises the process of signification by which the organism communicates.

The virus is symbiotic because in order to survive it has to invade a living organism and because the living organism is transformed (or killed) by the symbiotic agent. And the virus is sympoetic, in as much as it is symbolically coevolving with the social organism of the human.

Haraway uses the word *sympoiesis* to define reciprocal acts of creation in a process involving different living entities.

The pandemic virus has triggered a process of cultural and psychic mutation, but the mutation is not fully predetermined: it has to be elaborated by psychoanalysis and also by that kind of semiocreation that is called poetry.

In order to anticipate and counter and dissolve a likely wave of psychological regression, we need to reinvent courtesy, to reshape the relations between desire and language, to perform a poetic reimagination of the conjunction of bodies.

8

Autistic Mindscape

'I can't speak for all autistic people, but I feel things more intensely. In a shopping centre there's all of those different noises coming from different angles – my brain can't process them quickly enough, and everything goes completely crazy. Being out in nature, the sounds are quite level and I find it easier with muted colours. Everything just works. It's not oppressive.'[1]

This declaration by Dara McAnulty, the author of *Diary of a Young Naturalist*, speaks volumes about the contemporary trend towards autistic pathologies.

The human mind has reached a sort of saturation, too much noise, too many nervous stimulations; some individuals (an increasing number of individuals) cannot take it anymore and crack, socially speaking. More and more people fall out of the circuit of communication because their brain can't process stimulations quickly enough, so stimulations become noise, painful distressing noise. And everything goes completely crazy.

Dara McAnulty speaks about himself as a person who was diagnosed with Asperger's syndrome when he was five.

I have not read his book, but I read his interviews: he speaks about the beauty of the Irish landscape, but also of his own intellectual work in the context of dealing with his autistic condition.

'That's been quite important to me because I try my best to learn about humans so I can make acceptable social interactions.'[2]

Possibly this is the most comprehensive definition of autism I have read so far: the autistic person is someone who does not understand the meaning of social interactions. So they try their best to 'learn about humans' so they can make acceptable interactions. This is a description of autism in terms of noise, in terms of saturation of attention. In this way I am talking about a concept of autism as an exceptional, marginal reaction to the acceleration of the info-sphere.

This is what autism was yesterday.

Here I want to reflect on how aspects of an autistic sensibility might shape our psychological states tomorrow, beyond the threshold that we are trespassing, a threshold marked by low-intensity trauma, sub-acute depression and a sort of fogging in emotional attention.

The scientific definition of the syndrome called autism is rather elusive, and elusive is the behaviour displayed by those people (particularly very young people) affected by autistic syndrome.

According to the National Institute of Mental Health,

Autism spectrum disorder (ASD) is a developmental disorder that affects communication and behavior …

People with ASD have:

- Difficulty with communication and interaction with other people
- Restricted interests and repetitive behaviors
- Symptoms that hurt the person's ability to function properly in school, work, and other areas of life

Autism is known as a 'spectrum' disorder because there is wide variation in the type and severity of symptoms people experience. ASD occurs in all ethnic, racial, and economic groups. Although ASD can be a lifelong disorder, treatments and services can improve a person's symptoms and ability to function. The American Academy of Pediatrics recommends that all children be screened for autism. All caregivers should talk to their doctor about ASD screening or evaluation ...

Not all people with ASD will show all behaviors, but most will show several.[3]

In my own aberrant reading of this text, this symptomatology could be read not as a diagnosis of an anomic behaviour but culturally as the description of a novus homo that has emerged from the marriage of techno-culture and financial capitalism.

If autism involves a lowering of cognitive empathy (struggling with social cues) alongside an overload of affective empathy (overwhelming intuitive empathy that causes internal shutdown), autism can be read as a cultural marker of the age of financial capitalism that will grow in prevalence during this shift from the age of acceleration to the age that follows the great slowdown.

The kind of behaviour loosely designated as autistic is going to be the new common ground of human perception in the wake of the viral trauma.

If you want to grasp an idea of what autism means you should not read a handbook of psychopathology but Octavia Butler's 1993 novel *Parable of the Sower*. A synopsis from Gloria Steinem:

> Its story begins in a future California that has become divided into three overlapping worlds ... It is in the middle population in walled communities, struggling to preserve a past order, that we meet a teenager called Lauren.
>
> She is our narrator. She is smart and subject to hope and fear, friends and betrayals. She's also afflicted with hyperempathy syndrome, something she inherited from her drug-addicted mother. It causes her to feel the pain of any living being around her, yet the pain may be so great that it immobilizes her, and she cannot help the one who is suffering [4]

Lauren's father is trying to convert her to the overall cynicism. The indispensable cynicism of those who are dwelling in an environment in which pain is so visible, so widespread.

> My father glanced back at me every now and then. He tells me, 'You can beat this thing. You don't have to give into it.' He has always pretended, or perhaps believed, that my hyperempathy syndrome is something I could shake off and forget about ...
>
> Hyperempathy is what the doctors call an 'organic delusional syndrome.' Big shit. It hurts, that's all I know. Thanks to the Paracetco ... the particular drug that my mother chose to abuse before my birth killed her, I'm crazy. I get a lot of grief that doesn't belong to me, and that isn't real, but it hurts.
>
> I'm supposed to share pleasure *and* pain, but there isn't much pleasure around these days.[5]

In this future world, those who are hypersensory are considered crazy, weak persons affected by the delusion of feeling pain (or occasionally joy) about others. Obviously in this hell it is better not to perceive the pain of those who surround you. Dealing with your own pain is painful enough.

Intuition about others, and fundamentally the intuition that others exist: this is an assumption that we generally take for granted.

According to neurophysiologist Vittorio Gallese, our brains are endowed with nervous cells (*mirror neurons*, in his parlance) that make it possible to recognise others and the meaning of their behaviours.

Marco Iacoboni, a neuroscientist at the University of California, Los Angeles, views mirror neurons as the neural basis of the human capacity for emotions such as empathy. Notably there are differences between cognitive empathy and affective empathy.

Also, this neural basis is just a precondition for a wide range of degrees of empathy. Emotion and culture are mutually influencing, and in the cultural threshold that we are trespassing the emotional spectrum is going to mutate.

This mutation is not determined, because the threshold is the place of an oscillation. Autism is an emerging trend of the emotional spectrum, and I see the danger that a lack of cognitive empathy is going to be an attractive pole of the emotional spectrum in the pandemic mutation and its aftermath.

We are facing an unprecedented burden of suffering, and a new generation might be naturally refusing responsibility for what is happening in a world they have not chosen to inhabit and to accept the suffering of the others (through cognitive empathy) as something of common concern.

Alexithymia might be a consequence of this burden of suffering: research indicates that alexithymia overlaps with autism spectrum disorders (ASD). The inability to name emotions, to feel the presence of the other as something emotionally relevant, is the main legacy of the shift from conjunction to connection.

The difficulty in identifying feelings and the difficulty in describing feelings are also significantly associated with symptoms of hyperactivity/impulsivity.

9

XXX

What is the message of *Anti-Oedipus*, the book that captured the attention of many young activists and scholars in the 1970s? What did we find in that book? The promise of the liberation of desire, or the announcement of a coming entrapment of desire in the neoliberal rhizomatic whirlwind? Or both?

In my opinion, the message of *Anti-Oedipus* is that desire is the main field of social becoming; that arena of conflict and progress, of oppression and of liberation. But desire is not the good guy, is not a progressive force and an enlightening energy. It is a field of contention that may nurture opposed projects.

As the viral storm is ravaging the field of desire, we cannot predict the evolution of the erotic sensibility: the only thing we can do is gauge the depth of the disturbance and fathom how sensibility can reorient desire.

Kisses

'Skip kissing and consider wearing a mask when having sex to protect yourself from catching the coronavirus, Canada's chief medical officer said ... adding that going solo remains the lowest risk sexual option in a pandemic.'[1]

For the first time in history we are invited to abstain from kissing. In the worst-case scenario you are invited to wear a mask while having sex, and preferably you are invited to do it yourself.

One may observe that abstaining from kissing is only a marginal annoyance, when millions of people are going to lose their jobs because of the pandemic.

I don't agree.

I'm not going to discuss the medical benefits of these kinds of suggestions – maybe they are necessary for reducing the lethal impact of the virus.

Nevertheless, I think that a phobic sensibilisation to the lips and skin of the other is a danger that goes beyond the immediate consequences of the pandemic: a danger of a dis-eroticisation of the social relation, a danger of inhibiting the most elementary act of bodily relaxation that mitigates the pain of being alive.

'Kisses and hugs' are the final words of almost every e-message I have sent in the months of the lockdown.

Virtual kisses, sent from a keyboard to a distant screen.

Meanwhile the physical three-dimensional event of lips approaching has been suspended, the proxemics that prelude the contact of lips and tongues has been enveloped in shadows of fear, of respect, of caution.

Among all the human acts the kiss seems to be the most human, so it's easy to imagine that something is going to happen in the unconscious dimension of sensuousness.

Man is not the only animal capable of communication: thanks to chemical transmission ants send each other information about very complicated matters, and bees direct the flight of their sisters with abdominal vibrations.

However, as far as I know, no animal approaches the lips of the other with its own lips, tilting the head in a delicate suggesting way, no animal caresses with the tongue the internal parts of the mouth, sipping sweetness from the other's palate. Only humans know the language of kisses, which flawlessly communicate the inexplicable chemistry of pleasure and desire.

Not all human cultures have used exactly the same technique – some populations may like to rub their noses, some do even more exotic queernesses. However, even if I don't want to appear ethnocentric, let me say that kissing is beautiful.

On 9 May 2020, the *Economist* published an editor's note:

Social distancing makes meeting in the flesh hard ...

The solitude of lockdown is making [people] reconsider what they want from romantic relationships.

Nearly 240m people use dating apps and websites. Even before the pandemic American couples were more likely to meet each other through online-dating services than through personal contacts, according to a study published in 2019 by sociologists from Stanford University and the University of New Mexico ...

In April the average number of messages sent daily across Match products, including OkCupid, PlentyOfFish, Tinder, Hinge and Match.com, was up by 27% compared with the last week of February. During the worst week of China's epidemic, in late February, the average user of TanTan, a Chinese app, spent 30% longer on the app than normal ...

Zoom chats with friends and family have become routine in the age of Covid-19. Some 70% of American singles surveyed by Match said they would now use video ...

And people are surprisingly willing to bare their souls on video dates ...

Until people need no longer worry about Covid-19, most singletons will be wary of close contact with potential mates. Almost all OkCupid users, polled since March, say they plan to continue using video. The virtual date may outlast the pandemic.[2]

Of course virtual dates will outlast the pandemic.

Until people need no longer worry about Covid-19 they will be wary of close contact, they will be wary of the exchange of saliva, they will be wary of kisses. But this wariness is not going to disappear when the World Health Organization declares that coronavirus is defeated. First of all, because we have now entered a pandemic age, in which the spread of contagious diseases might be a permanent threat. Second, because this experience is going to leave an imprint in sensitivity well beyond the rational measures of medical self-protection.

In an article for the *New York Times*, filmmaker Nayeema Raza writes, 'While kissing is the most effective way to gauge chemistry, it's also the most efficient way to contract the coronavirus.'[3]

Raza then attempts to extract some moral lessons from our experiences of living through the pandemic:

> We're starting to have conversations about coronavirus status, quarantine credentials and exclusivity that are as awkward as our first virtual dates. These kinds of conversations aren't unprecedented. New couples navigate them in any relationship, often around safe sex. Now we'll have these intimate conversations for something as innocent as a first kiss. If we want to be safe, we have to.
>
> As the world opens up, we might start dating more selectively, more slowly, more sequentially, with more anticipation and attention than we have in years …
>
> And let's be honest, there's something a little thrilling about a first kiss being taboo again.
>
> Maybe we needed that.[4]

I don't like Raza's frivolous and somewhat reactionary tone here, as she hints that the virus – while not exactly a punishment for the permissiveness of sex culture – is a sort of reminder, a moral correction of sorts.

Should we go back to mandatory monogamy, should we be suspicious of those who do not belong to the family? Is this the cultural outcome?

I don't want to invite anybody to superficiality or recklessness, but I think that the fear of approaching cheek to cheek and lip to lip is worse than the nuclear bomb for human future happiness.

I know, this is an exaggeration, once more. I do it sometimes, maybe too often.

But I think that hyperbole is the best way to go to the heart of a problem, and I think that a painful impoverishment of erotic experience may be in sight.

Eros in Danger

Awareness about the weakening of sexual drives among the population of the Northern Hemisphere is not new. In 2015 Professor David Spiegelhalter published *Sex by Numbers*, a book about the sexual disaffection of the latest generation of Americans.

More recently a survey published by *JAMA Network Open* assesses that 'US adults (aged ≥18 years) had sexual frequencies of approximately 9 fewer times per year in the early 2010s compared with the late 1990s.'[5]

Is sex disappearing? Actually it is not, because the disastrous increase in world population is not stopping, at least not in non-Western countries. And the political authorities of Europe are worrying over the constantly decreasing birth rates among white people, so governments are investing money to persuade women to procreate, and contribute to the national glory. At the global scale reproduction does not stop, even if it is a trend no less dangerous than air pollution.

In *Staying with the Trouble*, feminist philosopher Donna Haraway expresses worries about the dramatic effects of the predictable growth of the population of the world, and remarks how the subject is delicate, particularly from a feminist point of view:

Food, jobs, housing, education, the possibility of travel, community, peace, control of one's body and one's intimacies, health care, usable and woman-friendly contraception, the last word on whether or not a child will be born, joy: these and more are sexual and reproductive rights. Their absence around the world is stunning. For excellent reasons, the feminists I know have resisted the languages and policies of population control because they demonstrably often have the interests of biopolitical states more in view than the well-being of women and their people, old and young. Resulting scandals in population control practices are not hard to find. But, in my experience, feminists, including science studies and anthropological feminists, have not been willing seriously to address the Great Acceleration of human numbers, fearing that to do so would be to slide once again into the muck of racism, classism, nationalism, modernism, and imperialism.

But that fear is not good enough. Avoidance of the urgency of almost incomprehensible increases in human numbers since 1950 can slip into something akin to the way some Christians avoid the urgency of climate change because it touches too closely on the marrow of one's faith ... A 9 billion increase of human beings over 150 years, to a level of 11 billion by 2100 if we are lucky, is not just a number; and it cannot be explained away by blaming Capitalism or any other word starting with a capital letter.[6]

Falling birth rates are affecting large parts of the world, but they are matched by population increases in other areas. However, those migrating from high-birth-rate poor countries are rejected by low-birth-rate rich populations. Therefore, the much-needed redistribution of the world's population, that actually would be a common interest, is actively crippled just because the redistribution hurts the white senile instinct of self-protection.

The Italian population has been ageing for years and the trend is steady. Birth rate has been declining constantly.

Nevertheless, in the last thirty years various governments have been adamant in pursuing an antimigration policy: containment, detention, rejection have favoured the exploitation of migrants who are made illegal by absurd legislation, then reduced to a slave workforce.

European countries like Poland, France and Italy have decided to give money to women who give birth to a child. I dare to say that these are sinister acts of racism and female abasement. The white race is paying to rent your womb, as you procreate white children for the nation.

Obviously women (and men) sometimes desire to have a child.

But in the world there are plenty of children who have no mother, no food, and are waiting for parents.

What motivation can push you to make a child out of your body?

Just ponder: demographers expect the population to rise from nine to eleven billion people on Earth during this century. Water is in short supply in many areas of the planet. Climate change is going to shrink inhabitable space in the coming decades. Last but not least: the underlying message of the virus is that safety lies in lowering human-to-human contact.

More people, less space, less distance, more contagion.

If the demographic trend is confirmed, extinction looms.

I know how controversial is my consideration on the catastrophic effects of the demographic trends, I understand how dangerous and almost impracticable any political intervention on this subject would be, but I think that the silence of intellectuals and activists on this point would be hypocritical and guilty. Religious persons think that giving birth is always an act of love, but I think, on the contrary, that giving birth to someone who will almost certainly go through an age of misery and despair is not an act of love; it is an act of evil.

I'm not calling for political control on procreation, as I also think that authoritarian intervention would be unacceptable and would not stop the demographic trend. But every reasonable person knows that the expected increase in the world population (that might reach the frightening number of ten or eleven billion before a downturn of the curve) would be a final blow to human life on a planet that is shrinking because of climate change.

Let's go back to sex. We have seen that sex is not disappearing in the world, just fading in the northern part of the planet. But if sex is not dead, Eros is the casualty of the converging attack of virtual technology and viral invasions.

What is the meaning of the word *eroticism*? Freud distinguishes between *Instinkt* and *Trieb* (instinct and drive). In his understanding, erotic experience is based upon this distinction. Animals are driven by instinct – that allows for reproduction. But human sexuality is not limited to the pursuit of reproduction, far from it. Desire is not aimed towards reproduction but towards knowledge. Exceeding the self is the core of sexual drive: desire to be traversed by flows of the other, to inhale the other, to smell the flavour of the other, to lick the skin of the other, to become the other.

When Georges Bataille speaks of eroticism in terms of excess, he means that eroticism is not responding to needs, to necessities, is not complying with self-preservation, is not helping survival. It is just responding to the desire of seeing what we have not seen, of touching what is not allowed, the desire of putting the self at risk. Eros is knowledge of what is irreducible to knowledge, of what exceeds your attempts at reduction. The unknown that ceaselessly is exposing itself to your capture and ceaselessly escaping your capture.

This is what we know of eros: that it is the hide-and-seek game of the unknown, the possession of shadows, the neverending irredeemable experiences of joy and delusion that help Sisyphus to start again start again start again.

Now, however, we are led to rethink desire, eroticism and sexuality in the shadow of this threshold, trepidly waiting for an aftermath that is visible in the light of the outside as a quivering mirage.

From these uncertain considerations I have developed some mental meanderings, inconsistent as all such digressions are.

Sisyphus

My first digression is about the myth of Sisyphus, particularly as manifested in Albert Camus's revisitation.

As you remember, Sisyphus is forced to push a heavy stone up a slope. When he has reached the top of the hill, the stone rolls back down along the declivity, so he must go down and start his fatigue-inducing labour again.

Camus writes, 'It is during this descent, during this pause, that Sisyphus is interesting to me. I see this man descending slowly toward the torment that will never end.'[7]

Camus's conclusion, however, is that we should imagine that Sisyphus is happy, because his hopeless action reveals the absurdity of the human condition and also reveals that this absurd condition can be shared with others who are suffering the same curse.

'Where is the meaning of life?' wonders Camus, and he replies: in the realisation that meaning is nowhere. Life will be better if we know that it has no meaning, no reason, no aim. This does not mean despair, but freedom, rebellion with no goal: the negation of God and of eternity, the negation of the Absolute, as the finality is not contained in destiny or duration of life, but hidden in the intensity of days.

So a question arises: How can we live happily within a condition that has no goal, no transcendent finality, no stable certainty? And my answer is this: we can because we share our lives with wonderful creatures who are both like us and different, because together we are pushing uphill the stone of history, and together we go downhill and start again and again, from the beginning. But during that slow descent, we utter inebriating words and kiss each other on the mouth.

Look at the rebels who fought against the monsters. Monsters came again into sight, some of them emerging from the ranks of the rebels themselves.

But rebels do not despair – they are happy because they like each other, and hug each other, and their rebellion is rhythmically punctuated by kisses and caresses.

How will we accept the absurd violences of history if we'll be prevented from coming physically close?

10

Sad Is Eros

And Weeping Anarchic Aphrodite

Just after Freud's death, W. H. Auden wrote a poem devoted to him that oscillates between a sense of resigned wisdom and the perception of an imminent tragedy.

We are in 1939, the Second World War is beginning and the poet is acutely aware of its apocalyptic implications.

Freud is the Jewish exile who dies in London just when Europe sinks into the most frightening of abysses, and the poet describes him as someone who has enlightened the pathway of mankind just as it is on the brink of a catastrophe.

> Only Hate was happy, hoping to augment
> his practice now, and his dingy clientele
> who think they can be cured by killing
> and covering the garden with ashes.[1]

Freud's death is received with joy by the preachers of hate: psychoanalysis is a dialogic way to dissolve the inmost monsters that generate hate.

The fascist regimes that in those years were preparing the devastation of Europe are the dingy clientele of those who resort to killing as a cure for their pain, those who want to fight monsters by turning into monsters.

Now we know that the dingy clientele did not disappear after the crumbling of fascism: it has resurrected under neoliberal clothes and is spreading all over the world.

Nationalism and racism have grown invasive and are holding the reins of the fake beacon of democracy, America. The relation between mental pain, madness and dementia is clear in that country where 67,000 people died in 2018 from overdoses from opioid medication and where every day 319 people are shot, and of those 106 people are killed.[2]

Auden suggests in this text that power fears psychoanalysis because it's aim is to essentially liberate individuals from conformism and subjection.

> One rational voice is dumb. Over his grave
> the household of Impulse mourns one dearly loved:
> sad is Eros, builder of cities,
> and weeping anarchic Aphrodite.[3]

Beyond its therapeutic function, how can psychoanalysis act upon the process of conscious subjectivation? What is the contribution of psychoanalyses to the collective mental evolution during apocalyptic situations, like the one described by Auden, and like the one we are living through today?

In order to find an answer to this question, I'll delve into the subject of sublimation: a word that Freud briefly introduces in his writings but one that has not been investigated in its philosophical implications, as far as I know.

As political will cannot stop the spread of a virus, and as the virus jeopardises physical proximity, the space of psychoanalysis is reframed, if we think of it not only as individual therapy but also as a conscious shaping of social expectations, of the rhythm of collective breathing.

Sublimation and Its Discontents

In his works, and particularly in *Three Essays on the Theory of Sexuality*, Freud speaks of sublimation as the faculty to exchange the original sexual goal with another, no more sexual, but psychologically akin to the former.

In terms of affective economy, the concept of sublimation explains the dynamics that lead to activities that have no direct relation to sex but have the ability to absorb and catalyse sexual energy: art, poetry, philosophy, spiritual life, moral choice, scientific research and broadly speaking the entire process of civilisation.

These activities draw their energy from a transformation, a translation of sexual desire towards goals that are not directly sexual.

Sublimation in Freud plays the role of protecting from anxiety: as civilisation implies the denial of a large part of our sexual imagination, says Freud in *Civilization and Its Discontents*. The energy coming from that original drive has to be diverted and invested in a direction that is different from erotic pleasure and from the bodily discharge of tension.

The postponement and displacement of sexual desire does not occur without a psychological price being paid: neurotic pathology is the price of civilisation. Sublimation, in the Freudian context, acted as a protection from anxiety, and repressed energies could be invested in a direction different from libidinal satisfaction.

Three steps are implied in this displacement: the first is removal (*Verdrängung*), the second is libidinal displacement, and the third is sublimation as linguistic creation. But this displacement may have a repressive effect giving way to neurotic pathology.

In fact, some anti-authoritarian thinkers on psychoanalysis (Wilhelm Reich and Erich Fromm, Herbert Marcuse and Guattari, amongst others) react to the notion of sublimation with a certain suspicion, because sublimation may be seen as a way to repress desire, by diverting it towards less immediate and selfish goals.

The question is how the removal-displacement mechanism can result in creative sublimation rather than pathogenic repression.

Sublimation may be intended as a surrogate, an *Ersatz*, but it may be intended also as a consciously shared rewiring of desire, a cultural elaboration of desire at a new level.

The neoliberal acceleration and the 'just do it' culture have impoverished the ability to sublimate. People have been incited to consume more and more, to rapidly draw pleasure from homologated experience, and to enjoy as fast as possible as much as possible. Pure pulsional discharge, no emotional elaboration. In such conditions the ability of sublimation shrinks. The repression demanded by the pandemic slowdown generates an aggressive negation of reality.

Furthermore, sublimation has acquired a new dimension in the digital sphere, as the connective mutation enables and enforces the sterilisation of contacts and replaces touching with phantasmagory, pleasure with unending excitement.

The pandemic enhances contactless communication and therefore paves the way to the final automation of language, to the final freezing of empathy.

In an article published by the *Guardian* in April 2020, Ciara Gaffney asks what sex life will become like. What about sex in the months of confinement, especially for the younger generation, of the so-called generation Z (as for Zoom)? She writes:

> It's with an almost nascent nostalgia that I recall the coining of the Gen Z 'sexual recession': a patronizing concern that our youngest generation would be rendered psychosexually stunted, unable or unwilling to fornicate due to over-exposure to smartphones, social media and porn.

To an extent, the stats affirmed this; between 1991 and 2017, the number of high school students having sex dropped from 54% to 40%. But in the nick of time, a worldwide pandemic arrived, and a budding sexual renaissance emerged in its wake.[4]

The bizarre thesis of Ciara Gaffney's article is that the pandemic is creating the conditions for a new sexual revolution, the core of which would be the development of a contactless sensitivity:

The rose-colored epoch before the coronavirus bitterly shamed the sending of nudes. They were perceived as gauche, even pathetic. In the lockdown era, however, thirst traps and nudes are not only making a glorious, unrepentant comeback, but are now a form of emboldened agency in Gen Z's blossoming sexual liberation ...

Stratified by distance, Gen Z is similarly tasked with reinventing what sex looks like, in a quarantined world where physical sex is frequently impossible. As free love shattered the conventions of its time, Gen Z's sexual renaissance is doing the same for organic sexual connection.[5]

I am reminded of the cybersex imagination that was around in the '80s and '90s. It's quite likely that in the near future, virtual reality technology will develop new forms of distant stimulation and sexual pleasure. But this is not the focus of Gaffney, who writes, 'Quarantine not only encourages, but forces, the prosperity of sexual exploration; of experimenting with nudes, thirst traps, camming and sexting for debauchery, mostly without IRL [In Real Life] repercussions.'[6]

Thirst trap means: traps that make you thirsty – all right, but what if there is no water?

The transmission and reception of sensual stimuli in virtual reality may have a useful function from a demographic point of view, as it would finally prevent procreation, at least for the next hundred years. But I don't think that a universe of pleasure can exist with no epidermis-to-epidermis contact, with no ironic wink at a very close distance, with no sense of smell.

Meanwhile, in the *New York Times*, Julie Halpert writes about the spread of panic attacks among young Americans, who are locked up at home and exposed to a nonstop information flow.[7]

The proxemic alteration enforced by the pandemic is changing the perception of the body of the other, and this may generate temporary suffering and also permanent alterations in bodily sensibility, but also new forms of cultural sublimation.

During the lockdown and also after the lockdown, as the contagion persists as a looming danger, we have displaced affective relations into the virtual sphere. Also courtship, erotic exchanges have been virtualised with ambiguous effects.

The displacement of erotic communication from the dimension of physical presence to the dimension of language and images may result in quiet sublimation, but it also may result in depressive frustration.

The emotional intensity that absent communication arouses is mounting and mounting in a sort of vacuum up to the point of intolerable anxiety.

I'm violently desiring bodies that I cannot touch, that I cannot smell. The body is revealed in an emotional presence that does not evolve into physical presence, into touch. Depressive anxiety is a possible outcome of this situation.

Courtesy

The authors of *A Thousand Plateaus* propose that what we need is nomadism, the contrary of history. In his last book, Guattari says that contemporary history is more and more marked by the rise of identitarian reterritorialisations of subjectivity.

A certain universalist representation of subjectivity, based on Western colonialism, has failed, but the scale of this failure has not been fully appreciated so far. The pandemic threshold is obliging us to ponder the effect of those dark energies that follow the disintegration of enlightened universalism. The resistance against this disintegration assumes identitarian forms that emerge in racism, nationalism, fundamentalism.

Reasoning about identity, I want to go back to the historical origins of the modern perception of belonging, and in order to do this I'll say something about the concept of aristocracy, and about the opposing meanings that can be attributed to this concept.

Aristocracy (the power of the best) is originally based on the social privilege of belonging, blood purity, a direct relation with an origin (ethnical, religious, national, and so on), but the word *aristocracy* is not necessarily linked to this narrow definition.

In European precapitalist countries at the end of the Middle Ages, during a time of religious wars, ethnic contamination and territorial displacements, aristocracy emerged as the representation of purity, of noncontamination, of direct relation with an origin, and therefore with truth. But in the course of time, *aristocracy* acquired a different, almost opposite meaning.

Not truth, but knowledge is the issue of the second aristocracy, the aristocracy of courtesy, contamination and love.

In Europe this divergence happened in the centuries of the *cultura cortese*, whose sources can be found in Andalusia, Sicily, Catalonia, Provence and Tuscany, where the contamination of Muslim, Christian and Jewish culture nurtured the modern revolution of subjectivity.

In the Seminar VIII, where he speaks of sublimation, Jacques Lacan distinguishes between the premodern sexuality, in which drive (*Trieb*) is the focus of eros, and modern sexuality, in which the object of desire (the beloved person) is the focus of the erotic emotion.

The aristocratic principle of devotion to the King, to the Church, to the Pope and to God is matched and recoded by a new principle of devotion: the devotion to love (*fedeltà d'amore*).

In *Love in the Western World*, Denis de Rougemont identifies this divergence in the courtly romance novel par excellence: Tristan, the story of a nobleman who is charged to bring Isolde – the promised spouse of his king, Mark – from Ireland. During the journey, Tristan and Isolde fall in love, due to a magic potion representing the irresistibility of passion.

The divergence between devotion to the king and devotion to love will bring Tristan and Isolde unspeakable sufferings, unspeakable pleasures and finally death.

The feudal concept of aristocracy is subverted: while the blood aristocracy praises closure and purity as the mark of social and spiritual superiority, the courteous (or courtly) aristocracy praises especially promiscuity, contamination, availability to what Deleuze defines as 'becoming other'.

Christian culture emphasised individuality and introspection, so in the Christian sphere the narrative of courtly love led to modern romanticism: this thread is the erotisation of knowledge.

Curiosity for the singularity is the trigger of desire, and knowledge of the singularity is the core of erotic pleasure.

The poetic and anthropological revolution that paved the way to humanistic culture is this: in the traditional-patriarchal time, knowledge is viewed as restepping towards the origin, as an obsessional protection of an original truth constantly exposed to the risk of dispersion, the courteous feminisation of poetry and behaviour. The revolution announced a new way of thinking and perceiving, that knowledge is exactly this: dispersion of the self, dissolution of identity, experience of the unknown.

The mad flight (*folle volo*) of Dante's Ulysses marks this point of subversion; knowledge is becoming other.

The Renaissance, the scientific revolution, the very dynamics of modernity, presuppose this subversion of the relation between knowledge and alterity.

What is courtesy at the end of the day? I would say that courtesy is the linguistic evolution of desire, the elaboration of drive into language: courtship. That means that aristocracy is no more the class of the purest, but a coterie of those who can understand each other, even if they do not share the same lineage: linguistic intention takes the place of ontological origin. Permeability takes the place of integrity.

The concept of community (*Gemeinschaft*) is at stake here, in its opposition to *Gesellschaft* – a negotiated participation in a supercommunitarian political entity: the national State, the institutionalised society. The late modern evolution has dissolved this sense of *Gemeinschaft* and enforced the sense of conventional integration of society and in the end the universal dependence on monetary abstraction: *Gesellschaft*.

This process of deterritorialisation and of destruction of the community has been brought to the extreme by the globalisation of the last few decades. But we know that any deterritorialisation also puts in motion reactive processes of territorialisation. So, in the wake of the immense anthropological and psychological turmoil unleashed by globalisation, the disintegration of the living continuum of community has provoked a worldwide reactionary movement, and the idea of community has come back, charged with ambiguousness, because *community* is a concept as ambiguous as the word *aristocracy*.

There is a nomadic community that is based on the conscious sharing of intellectual and aesthetic values, a community that gathers abruptly and abruptly disperses, a community of people who stay in the same place as long as desire holds them together.

And there is a community of belonging, based on the illusion of a common origin and a common territory. This community (race, homeland, family, and so on) feeds authoritarianism, patriarchalism and war.

The nomadic kind of community does not protect its borders, because it does not protect its identity. It's essentially dispersive and pursues proliferation. It is not based on identity and fosters a dissipation of social, cultural and ethnic identifications.

Marx stated that the main goal of proletarian struggle is the abolition of the proletarian class. Similarly we may say that the goal of nomadic community is becoming other, to dissolve its identity, to forget about origins. In fact, the nomadic community is simultaneously elective and dispersive. It is elective because it is based on choice and desire, and it is dispersive because it aims to proliferate.

But if kisses turn into a threat, a spectre of unconscious fear, don't you see the danger that the very source of energy that moves us to action, to knowledge and to adventure will be severed? This is my main theoretical concern in the present threshold.

In the past three decades the psychotic explosion of the unconscious provoked by the great acceleration has jeopardised the erotic sphere. Porn has invaded the erotic imagination, visual stimulation has replaced bodily contact. But now, in the wake of the pandemic, we are pushed beyond that limit, as a new constellation of sensibility is taking shape: What can we glimpse beyond the threshold? A decreasing of the intensity of desire, a spread of depression and autism? Or a creative displacement of the pulsional energy?

Part III

Becoming Nothing

11

Mythology of the End

Apocalypses without Eschaton

In 1977 an unfinished book was published, *La fine del mondo* (the end of the world), that the Italian anthropologist Ernesto De Martino was writing when death took him away.

In 2019 I read the new enhanced edition of the book, edited by Giordana Charuty, Daniel Fabre and Marcello Massenzio.

I had first read the book at the end of the '70s, when I was having an initial glimpse of the possibility of the world's end – just because my own world was collapsing.

Reading the new edition just before the beginning of the contagion that is announcing the end of the world on a larger scale, I have been obliged to compare the present apocalyptic sentiment with the apocalyptic sentiment that was embedded in the movement of '77 in which I took part.

In that year we chanted the slogan '*A poco a poco Apocalisse*' (little by little Apocalypse) as a promise of revenge. In London, punk artists were chanting 'No future'.

Forty years after the said revenge has come, and the void of the future is on display, because the destructive forces of nature are erupting, and the global mind is collapsing.

In his unfinished book, De Martino distinguishes two different modes of apocalyptic imagination that converge in a psychotic perception of the vanishing of our world.

The first mode refers to an eschatological prospect, like the Christian apocalypse that is simultaneously revelation, judgement and salvation. Also communist apocalypses contain an eschatological vision: the Hegelian *Aufhebung*, the final establishment of a society without classes, without alienation, and therefore fully human.

However, De Martino's main focus is on apocalypses without eschaton, the one that we are facing now, after the dissolution of the communist perspective and after the dissolution of the potency of voluntary acts of decision.

Nevertheless, the first thing that De Martino does is explain what is the world whose end we can imagine:

> The world can finish because human civilisation has created the condition for self-annihilation: loss of the meaning of the intersubjective values of human life. The very potencies of technical domination can be employed towards a goal that is essentially devoid of meaning – that is, the annihilation of the very possibility of culture. The most essential mark of our age is the consciousness that the world can be terminated.[1]

By the word *world* De Martino intends to convey a cultural context that provides meaning to the common experience. Therefore the end of the world consists in the dissolution of the cultural context that makes experience meaningful, sharable.

This possibility of dissolution takes an unprecedented form in the late modern age, the age that follows Hiroshima, but also the age that follows the capitalist devastation of the planet's environment.

However, even if this technical manifestation of the apocalypse without eschaton is unprecedented, the end of the world has already happened during the history of humankind, under different forms.

The thorough destruction of the Amerindian culture, for instance, is a story that fully pertains to the definition of apocalypses without eschaton. Many ends of the world have happened in the many places where European colonialism has destroyed the possibility of attributing meaning to existing forms of life and communication.

Colonialism has already provoked many ends of the world. Why should we be surprised if the final collapse of colonialism (that some call postcolonialism) coincides with the end of the world itself?

The movement Extinction Rebellion first appeared in the United Kingdom, then spread through many countries in the Northern Hemisphere. It confronted the problem of the multiplicity of world endings when activists of Wretched of the Earth, a coalition of climate justice groups, opened a discussion with this letter:

> For many, the bleakness is not something of 'the future'. For those of us who are indigenous, working class, black, brown, queer, trans or disabled, the experience of structural violence became part of our birthright. Greta Thunberg calls world leaders to act by reminding them that 'Our house is on fire'. For many of us, the house has been on fire for a long time: whenever the tide of ecological violence rises, our communities, especially in the Global South are always first hit.[2]

The peoples of the Global South, the native people of the American continent, the Australian aboriginals, the African communities hit by slave deportation, and many others have already known the experience of extinction, when colonisation destroyed the context in which common experience was meaningful.

Now the same process is underway on a global scale, and it takes two forms that may appear opposed but are complementary: on one hand, we have the dissolution of the universalist horizon and the multiplication of identitarian conflicts, and therefore panic eruptions, *marasma*, and global civil war.

On the other hand (in an opposing but converging way), we have the establishment of a connective all-pervading

Meta-Machine that enables the automation of meaning: the global cognitive automaton is the consequence of the insertion of linguistic automatisms in the connections of social communication.

The effect of these two converging processes is the end of the world. De Martino:

> In the religious history of mankind the theme of the end of the world appears in eschatological context, as a recurring cosmic palingenesis or as a result of the evil that is inherent to mundane existence ... Opposite to the eschatological prospect, the present conjuncture of the Western world meets the theme of the end out of any religious context of salvation, as hopeless catastrophe of the familiar, of the meaningful and operable: a catastrophe that meticulously narrates the dissolution of the configured, the estrangement of the familiar, the loss of meaning of the signifier, the inoperability of the operable.[3]

The Premonition

The years during which De Martino was writing *La fine del mondo* were for me years of premonition: a wide and multifarious cultural movement – affecting music, politics, art, lifestyles – outlined a collective presentiment of the dissolution of the modern promise, of the progressive prospect.

In Italy the premonition appeared in the movement that may be called the last proletarian revolutionary movement of the century, the movement of Autonomia that peaked in 1977 with an insurrection that was incomprehensible for the political mind.

In that same year Margaret Thatcher began the march towards the conquest of power and to the establishment of a new regime based on the dismantlement of social solidarity. In 1987 Thatcher declared, 'There's no such thing as society. There are individual men and women and there are families. And no government can do anything except through people, and people must look after themselves first. It is our duty to look after ourselves and then, also, to look after our neighbours.'4 That declaration marked the beginning of the destruction of social civilisation built during the twentieth century and the end of universal humanism.

During those years I travelled to America for the first time, and I experienced the exacerbated sensibility of the American no-wave culture and the mythologies of the end that were permeating the American (particularly the Californian) culture-scape. That cultural sensibility was at the time perceiving the buzzing of the Meta-Machine, of new linguistic technologies announcing the death of the alphabetical man.

In two different ways, Herbert Marcuse and Marshall McLuhan were the philosophical harbingers of that premonition.

The Doors and Jim Morrison were the soundtrack: 'This is the end, beautiful friend.'5

The Meta-Machine was not only buzzing in our ears, but it was also pulsating in our veins: the meta-machine heroin, substance that speaks through your body.

When the global '68 movement was defeated, heroin became the announcer of the end.

When you have in your ears the buzz of the Meta-Machine what begins is the end of the world.

The world, as an entirety of culturally decodable signs, comes to an end when we lose the ability to decipher the meaning of the entirety of those signs.

At that point the Meta-Machine (mind-changing technologies, mind-changing drugs) starts to speak to the world, but the world cannot speak to the Meta-Machine. At that point, operability and signification proceed only from the outside of the cultural domain – from a semiotic technology that cannot be controlled but is controlling you.

12

Questioning Senility

Techno Immortality

Since the tail end of the past century – when demographic trends showed a decrease in birth rate and an increase in the average age of populations – old people have become a target for advertisers and for the overall economic system. While young people are jobless and precarious, while average wages decline and society is impoverished, the so-called boomers are still enjoying the effects of their past solidarity and of the struggles of the workers' movement: good salaries and decent pensions, earned during a life of hard work in the times when social solidarity and class struggle enabled the improvement of life standards and the extension of life spans.

Consequently, old people are the only ones around with some money in their pockets: not so much, but enough. This is why the great corporations of finance, pharmaceuticals, psycho-pharma and tourism have invested in the new silver market and sponsored a culture of techno-immortality.

The essence of advertising consists in exploiting the weakness of these various psycho-social groups: to young precarious workers, advertisers promise a quiet existence and a happy marriage if only they take a loan that will entangle them for life in debt. And to silver-aged consumers, advertisers promise eternal sexual energy and luxurious vacations in crowded locations filled with fading, arteriosclerotic good guys.

A transhumanist ideology accompanies this advertising

style, inciting consumers to invest money in the immortality business: biotechnology, pharmacology, genetics.

The techno-deletion of ageing is flourishing in the global North, and private medical research has progressed in the field, while at the same time public healthcare has been cut, the consequences of which are clearly visible throughout the pandemic storm.

How far can techno-pharma restoration go? How far can the prosthetisation of organs reach; the insertion of the inorganic into the biological organism?

How far can the digital simulate the continuum of life?

The computer scientist and inventor Ray Kurzweil's answer to this question is clear-cut: there are no limits to the micro-miniaturisation of digital engines simulating the organic, so there are no limits to the immortalising correction. We'll enact the singularity, the techno-*Ersatz* of the body-mind, as soon as miniaturisation allows for the replacement of the body, and of brain itself.

I do not have doubts about the ability of medical science married with computing science and biotechnology of making enormous progress in this field, allowing for dramatic rejuvenating therapies. I understand the enormous economic interest in this field of innovation, especially because these kinds of advanced therapies are addressed to the richest layers of the social spectrum. However, I don't trust the transhumanist promise for two reasons: first because of the obvious classist nature of this promise, and second because of the reductionism that it implies. The idea that existence is reducible to the efficacy of the biological machine is totally oblivious of the intimately psychic feature of time, of the accumulation of past experience as stratification of mental time.

The techniques of rejuvenation assume the idea that ageing is about the weakening and damaging of cells, molecules, tissues and organs. So the problem is how to repair and replace those organs and tissues and cells.

But this idea reflects an incredibly poor and naive conception (also a slightly inhuman conception) of what experience is, of what time is and therefore of what ageing is.

Is Old Age Over?

MIT Technology Review in October 2019 proclaimed that old age is over.

According to researcher Juan Carlos Izpisúa Belmonte, ageing is '"nothing other than molecular aberrations that occur at the cellular level." It is, he says, a war with entropy that no individual has ever won.'[1]

In the same issue, David Adam asks, in the title of his article, 'What if Aging Weren't Inevitable, but a Curable Disease?' He writes,

> If this controversial idea gains acceptance, it could radically change the way we treat growing old …
>
> Since ancient times, aging has been viewed as simply inevitable, unstoppable, nature's way. 'Natural causes' have long been blamed for deaths among the old, even if they died of a recognized pathological condition. The medical writer Galen argued back in the second century AD that aging is a natural process.
>
> His view, the acceptance that one can die simply of old age, has dominated ever since. We think of aging as the accumulation of all the other conditions that get more common as we get older – cancer, dementia, physical frailty. All that tells us, though, is that we're going to sicken and die; it doesn't give us a way to change it …
>
> But a growing number of scientists are questioning our basic conception of aging. What if you could challenge your death – or even prevent it altogether? What if the panoply of diseases that strike us in old age are symptoms, not causes? What would change if we classified aging itself as the disease?

David Sinclair, a geneticist at Harvard Medical School ... argues [that medicine] should view aging not as a natural consequence of growing older, but as a condition in and of itself.[2]

Adam goes on to infer that drug research

has highlighted a key question about aging: Is there a common mechanism by which different tissues change and decline? If so, could we find drugs to target that mechanism instead of playing what Harvard's David Sinclair calls 'whack-a-mole' medicine, treating individual diseases as they emerge? He believes there is, and that he has found a stunning new way to rewind the aging clock.

In unpublished work described in his coming book *Lifespan*, he says the key to his lab's work in this area is epigenetics. This fast-moving field focuses on how changes to the way genes are expressed, rather than mutations to the DNA itself, can produce physiological changes such as disease. Some of the body's own epigenetic mechanisms work to protect its cells, repairing damage to DNA, for instance; but they become less effective with age. Sinclair claims to have used gene therapy to effectively recharge these mechanisms in mice, and he says he can 'make damaged optic-nerve cells young again' to restore sight to elderly blind animals.[3]

And finally, quoting Sinclair again, 'If aging were a treatable condition, then the money would flow into research, innovation, and drug development. Right now, what pharmaceutical or biotech company could go after aging as a condition if it doesn't exist?' It should be, he says, the 'biggest market of all'.[4]

Not only is this line of thought aimed at enhancing the life expectancy of the rich at the expense of the life expectancy of the poor – as the 'biggest market of all' – not accessible for everybody, but also I think that reducing senility to a malady that should be medicalised and healed implies a philosophical denial of death and also of the specificity of old age.

The medical task is to restore the functionality of the organism, that is known. But ageing is not only a downgrading, but essentially a becoming. The reduction of senility to mere downgrading is a philosophical mistake that leads to the erasure of consciousness, pleasure, desire from existence.

The passing of time implies a mental becoming that overcomes the present, dissolving it into memory, and also implies a psychological becoming that changes the perception of future.

Therefore senescence should not be viewed as a purely organic process, but as a psychological becoming that demands a philosophical understanding.

Clearly there is an analogy between digital culture based upon abstraction and mathematical exactitude and the transhumanist cult of immortality. Eternity is an intrinsic feature of mathematical perfection, and immortality is inherent to abstraction. It's easy to contextualise the denial of carnal perishability within the shadow of digital ideology. But life is not mathematic, because it develops in time and time is the source of entropy, of dissolution and of decay, and also, let's not forget, of wisdom.

Digital de-ageing is more than nostalgia; it's the extermination of time. And of wisdom.

Resentment

Many sources tell the story of Eos, the dawn goddess, who, in the forest where she once dwelled, met Ares the warrior god and made love to him.

Furious about this infidelity, Ares's fiancée, Aphrodite, punished Eos – condemning her to fall in love with mortal beings alone.

So Eos went every day wandering in the woods looking for handsome hunters to seduce.

One day she met Tithonus, a young man of extraordinary beauty and noble origins who wandered in the outskirts of the city of Troy.

Eos was so charmed by him that she went to talk to Zeus, asking him to grant immortality to her lover. Zeus said yes, and Tithonus was allowed to enjoy forever Eos's love. Forever? Not really, because in her naive infatuation Eos forgot that humans, unlike gods, have an unfortunate habit of growing old. This point did not occur in her mind, because gods do not know about ageing. What is youth if not being alive in itself?

Eos and Tithonus lived together in love for a long time, then Eos started feeling sadness when she became aware that the man was drying out, and shrinking, and losing his vigour, and his voice was flagging. Eos realised that she could not sleep with him anymore, so she placed her senescent lover in a contiguous room of her house, as if he were a sick child. Then she almost forgot about him; every morning she went around looking for fresh young men, and time passed.

One night she heard the sound of a distant voice, like a lament. She opened the door of Tithonus's room, but he was not there. She looked around, then she looked downward, and she saw an insect, a cicada maybe, and recognised her love in that small being. She put him in a cage and set down the cage close to the bed where, every night, she received her lovers. Every morning she fed Tithonus with leaves of grass and ambrosia, and at night the chirp of the cicada accompanied her dreams.

In the beautiful, painful novel *Casanova's Homecoming*, Arthur Schnitzler recounts the story of Casanova on the brink of old age. He was coming back from his travels, wishing to spend his last years in the city of Venice. During this journey, Casanova meets a couple of friends in the outskirts of Mantua, and in their house, he is introduced to the nineteen-year-old

Marcolina and the young officer Lorenzi, whom Casanova suspects to be the secret lover of Marcolina. The old Casanova is overcome with desire for the young woman and by his envy of the young man whose youth, beauty and arrogance are so similar to his own past qualities.

Thanks to Schnitzler, we discover the devilish and sordid face of masculine decay. Casanova is tired of his own adventurous life and his never-ending wanderings. In order to be accepted in his hometown, he agrees to be a spy for the Venetian police. What is left of him is only the ability to intrigue, to cheat, to plot. And a melancholic sense of nostalgia.

'On an island near Venice there is a convent garden where I last set foot several decades ago. At night, there, the scent is just like this.'[5]

That flavour is gone, that nocturnal lightness is gone forever, and can only be reminded by sorrow, and from this impotent sorrow resentment blossoms.

Re-sentiment: a painful coming back of a sentiment, the sensing again what did exist but does not exist anymore. The comeback of perceptual fragments that the senile nervous system is unable to authentically feel.

Senescence, Psychoanalysis and Conscious Passing Away

> O! Let me not be mad, not mad, sweet heaven!
> Keep me in temper: I would not be mad!
>
> William Shakespeare, *King Lear*

Arthur Schnitzler's fictional world overlaps in many ways with the Freudian perspective of introspection, but if Schnitzler stages senescence as an abyss of bitterness and cynicism, Freud never systematically dealt with growing old.

Psychoanalysts do not say much about senility.

Literature has recounted the countless facets of old age and the approaching of death: from Shakespeare to Chekhov to Svevo, from Dostoevsky to Verga, not to mention Schnitzler. Poets and novelists have richly described and analysed the loss of strength, the loss of cognitive consistency that accompanies old age. But psychoanalysts have been cautious, almost tight-lipped about the subject, since Freud wrote that psychoanalytic therapy does not apply to those persons who have reached the age of senility.

According to Freud, in an old mind, the unconscious material is too large for the short time that is left to the analysand. The labyrinth of memory is too intricate and wide to be sorted out in such a short period of time.

If I may, this is not a very convincing argument.

However there is another reading of Freud's denial on the matter that seems to me more persuading:

'The question of ageing', writes the psychoanalyst Henri Bianchi in *La question du vieillissement*, 'lies beyond the borders of psychoanalysis, because ... it is inscribed in actuality and in the reality of biophysics, in thermo-dynamics.'[6]

The problem is that ageing, while revealing crucial dimensions for psychoanalytical discourse, is based on a spurious ground that since its inception psychoanalysis intended to evade: neurology.

Freud started his new discipline by fundamentally abandoning the field of neurology and focusing instead on language and sex. Only by leaving behind the neurophysical roots of mental suffering could Freud establish a new field based on the conceptual creation of the Unconscious that cannot be reduced to physiology or neurology, as it belongs to the sphere of relations between language and sex.

Since Freud made this conceptual displacement, neurological problematics were not abolished at all, but they were removed from the visual field of analytical interpretation and therapy.

The psychoanalyst, as such, is not concerned with neurological questions, even if they do not deny their existence and their relevance. Those questions pertain to the sphere of another discipline that precedes psychoanalysis and continues to exist and progress after it but was put aside by Freud in order to see the special action of sex on language and of language upon sex.

Of course the discourse on ageing cannot ignore neurology, because time leaves a footprint that is not only linguistic or psychic but also physical: degradation of brain tissues, loss of perceptual definition, the material entropy of the body that affects sexuality, cognition, pleasure and desire.

A senile person's unconscious records not only psychological experiences but also the traces of a neurological deformation that affects cognitive competence and that acts on their very psychological state. From the chapter 'Aging and Neurological Diseases' in the volume *Senescence: Physiology or Pathology*:

> The aging process starts with subclinical changes at the molecular level. These include the accumulation of mutations, telomere attrition, and epigenetic alterations leading to genomic instability. Such defects multiply exponentially over time, resembling a 'snowball effect', and eventually leading to morphological and functional deterioration of the brain, including progressive neuronal loss, reduced levels of neurotransmitters, excessive inflammation, and disrupted integrity of vessels, followed by infarction and microbleeds. Additionally, the decreasing efficiency of DNA repair mechanisms increases the susceptibility to reactive oxygen species and spontaneous mutagenesis, resulting in age-related neoplasia.[7]

In the senescent mind something happens that psychoanalysts cannot see and cannot elaborate on, as it depends on the neurophysical matter that transcends the limits of psychoanalysis.

So should we leave the poor old man in the hands of malicious geriatric reductionism, to the prosthetic industry, to neuro-technology, and transhumanist nano-engineering?

If we investigate old age from the point of view of reparations (that Jonathan Franzen calls 'corrections'), we'll not grasp the inmost meaning of senility.

In fact, old age has something interesting to say that cannot be fully realised by the neurologist or the psychoanalyst. The philosopher, however, can understand that something.

The relation between psychoanalysis and neuroscience is a crucial subject of our time. Some ask the question: Will psychoanalysis survive the development of neuroscience, or will neuroscience definitively supplant the psychoanalytic endeavour?

I think that psychoanalysis is not doomed, but in order to survive and evolve it has to enhance its scope.

Neuroscience focuses on the deterministic processes of the physical brain, while psychoanalysis focuses on the activity of the mind out of any line of determination.

Nevertheless there is a larger field of investigation, a field that is thoroughly philosophical, and encompasses both mind and time, both structure and machine, both being and becoming.

Old age exceeds psychoanalysis and medical science, because the essential meaning of ageing is not being ill or restoring well-being. The essential meaning of ageing is Being. To be more accurate: Becoming.

If we can subtract senility to heteronomous definitions (senility is the lack of this or the decaying of that), we can finally understand that the philosophical meaning of ageing is the most radical form of becoming: becoming nothing.

Here I enter into the prospective of a free passing away, the acknowledgement of death as a friend. I see death as an individual act of freedom that brings to completion the experience of living and brings to emergence the consciousness of nothingness. But death is also a therapeutic metaphor for the whole of humankind, in the age of exhaustion.

Western culture has been extremely cautious in referring to death, up to the point that all references to this subject are obliterated in daily chat and erased from the sphere of political discourse. This denial has been brutally questioned by the pandemic, then the irruption of death in the public space has changed the terms of politics and the imagination of the social future.

Furthermore, the demographical trend of the West – that is, the ageing of the average population (the conjoined effect of the progress of medicine and of the fall in birth rates) – is provoking the collapse of the cult of youth that prevailed in the modern age.

The cultural change of the new century is not only the result of economic and technological transformations but also an effect of the neurophysical decay of the human brain.

The irruption of neurophysics in psychiatric discourse has been brutal since we have widely witnessed the drama of Alzheimer's disease. Senile dementia is not new, of course, but in the past it was a marginal phenomenon in social life: old people were so few and so marginal that dementia was hardly noticed, even appreciated as expression of divine inspiration. Recently the extension of the average lifetime, and the expansion of the aged population, have outlined a new social landscape: old people who are unable to heal themselves are growing in number up to the point of becoming a major social problem.

Armies of caretakers coming from Moldavia and Ukraine are crowding the streets of European cities, while armies of sons and daughters in their fifties and sixties are obliged to confront the tragedy of their old parents. Dementia catalyses depression, economic problems, anxiety and a sense of guilt.

The inability to think about death as free choice precludes the possibility of offering a choice to those people who are facing the gradual loss of consciousness but who are still conscious enough to make a choice.

The stigma of suicide has a religious origin (God is the owner of your life, my dear, so you must wait for His high decision), but it has been reasserted by the economic episteme: life is private property, and property cannot be dilapidated. Then you have also the left-oriented stigma: you cannot withdraw from the social link; you have to fight until the end, and so on... .

This multifarious bullshit makes unthinkable the autonomous choice when we are facing death.

Suicide (the killing of someone who is the killer of themself) is the name that all kinds of bigots (religious bigots, economic bigots and socialist bigots) use to define the choice of conscious passing away. This misnaming obliges people to suffer pain, humiliation and worse, the degradation of the self.

Suicide should not be the word, but a free passing away, tuning into the cosmic becoming.

13

Making Friends with Death

Are you willing to be made nothing?
dipped into oblivion?
If not, you will never really change.

D. H. Lawrence, 'Phoenix'

If I might, I would rewrite the above quote from Lawrence to read as follows:

Are you willing to be made nothing?
dipped into oblivion?
If not, you will never really understand.

Death is a taboo for the Western mind.

It has not always been, as Philippe Ariès argues in *Western Attitudes toward Death from the Middle Ages to the Present* (1974).

He makes the case that death displaced sex as the main taboo in modern times when it became hidden from public view, when the hospital replaced the family home as the place for passing away: the experience of dying became detached from the community, and emotion was replaced by medical management of the body.

Furthermore, Ariès cites the transformation in social perception: death became shameful and almost forbidden because of the suppression of emotion that characterises the puritanical culture of the West, and also because 'people began to believe that life is always happy or should always seem so'.[1]

Expressing sadness or emotional turmoil, Ariès argues, is likely to be equated with bad manners, mental instability and unnecessary morbidity.

Ariès remarks that this process of denial and social marginalisation of the experience of death started during nineteenth-century America for reasons that, in my opinion, deserve to be explained.

Capitalist culture in general, and particularly American culture, is based on the opposition of winning or losing, as a dominant obsession. If we identify winning with energy, aggressiveness, profit, then dying means losing. Losing life, first of all, and also losing in the competitive social game. The cult of energy (*energolatria*) is fundamental to the rise of the bourgeois hegemony and in the building of the modern economy. Youthful energy and aggressiveness are not mere forms of expression of individual character but the basic values of American culture, where the word *loser* is perceived as the worst of insults. Death is the ultimate humiliation. Let's not forget that the very etymology of the word *humiliation* is 'being forced to go back to the earth'. Humiliation is at the core of our relation with the overwhelming forces of the external world, both natural and social.

When the coronavirus pandemic started raging in the United States, denial became widespread, thanks to the political approach of President Trump and the behaviour of a large part of the population. Denial of weakness, of impotence, denial of the virus itself, have to be seen as the consequences of the obsession of winning and of the refusal of the idea that human will is impotent when viral chaos invades the public domain.

Consequently death regained visibility in the American landscape, as well as everywhere else in the world. At this point a reconsideration of the role that is played by death in the collective unconscious becomes urgent.

A question is imposing itself: Should we rebel against

extinction, or should we reframe our lifestyles and mental attitudes in the wake of extinction?

Facing unpreventable death with a relaxed mind is probably a precondition for surviving pandemics, and also for dispelling the shadow of planetary extinction. So this is an opportunity to think of death as a friend.

Death as a friend makes its appearance in the Christian psyche: in the *Cantico delle Creature*, Saint Francis of Assisi calls death his sister. But in that religious sentiment the dissolution of the mundane body is the condition of an ultra-mundane new life. I don't believe in ultra-mundane life. I think that the material stuff you are composed of is destined to last forever, in the perennial recombination of physical particles. But you are not those particles; you are the consciousness that emerges from the provisional precarious composition of those particles.

Nothingness is a nonexisting thing, in nature. Nothingness does exist only in your consciousness; actually it is the destiny of your consciousness, as your consciousness will disappear with the final decomposition of your material body.

Epicurus, on his side, looks at death with a radically materialistic spirit, when he says, 'Death is nothing to us. For what has been dissolved has no feeling, and what has no feeling is nothing to us.'[2]

In its effort to prolong the duration of life, modernity has slowly erased the imagination of nothingness and has promoted the removal of death from the field of daily consciousness. This removal is the very condition of a systemic culture that denies the limit and that draws its energy from this denegation: this system is called capitalism, the most accomplished (but not really accomplished) attempt to overcome death, to give birth to the eternity of the abstract product of the human work: value.

Modernity has therefore deeply internalised the rejection of death: death is a scandal because it is the irruption of nature into the domain of culture, the comeback of the denied naturality that language and political order have denied and capitalism has tried to erase.

The effects of this removal and denegation have slowly emerged in the late modern age and now are in full visibility: dementia, terror, environmental devastation, a delirium of eternity embodied in money, technology, abstraction.

Death and Consciousness

James Hillman is one of the few psychoanalysts who have thematised death from a critical and not only medical point of view. In his book *Suicide and the Soul* (1964), he writes, '*Promoting life has come to mean prolonging it ...* But life can be prolonged only at the expense of death.'[3]

'At the expense of death' means that the medical striving to prolong life at all costs has the effect of impoverishing death, of worsening the quality of death, of reducing death to a defeat.

Death is not a defeat; it has to be perceived as the perfection of consciousness, the triumph of consciousness upon reality. Dissolving into nothing, consciousness finally dissolves reality itself.

The task of psychoanalysts, says Hillman, should be to consciously inscribe death in existence, as in the unconscious there is no opposition among the two dimensions.

Psychoanalysis cannot be reduced to mere psychotherapy: it is something different; it is the dispelling of the delusion of eternity. It is the comprehension of nothingness as the perfection of conscious existence.

In *The Force of Character: And the Lasting Life* (1999), Hillman takes a different stance, less radical and more pragmatic than before. He suggests that growing old helps character to emerge, finally free of its superstructures. This thesis does not fully persuade me.

In the first chapter of the book, the meaning of the word *character* is explained:

> A human body is like that sock, sloughing off its cells, chang-
> ing its fluids, fermenting utterly fresh cultures of bacteria as
> others pass away. Your material stuff through time becomes
> altogether different, yet you remain the same you. Not one
> square inch of visible skin, not one palpable ounce of bone is
> the same, yet you are not someone different. There seems to be
> an innate image that does not forget your basic paradigm and
> that keeps you in character, true to yourself. The idea of DNA
> seems too tight to hold the psychic dimensions of our unique
> image.[4]

The various schools of psychology use different words for *character*, such as *personality, ego, self, behavioural organisation, integrative structure, identity, temperament*. These substitute terms fail to characterise the styles of assimilation that are the hallmarks of individuality. *Ego, self, identity* are bare abstractions, telling us nothing of the human being they supposedly inhabit and govern. At best, these words refer to the unifying sameness of people while neglecting their unique differences.

Character, on the contrary, is what persists of a person, when every bodily feature changes: material components of the body (organs, tissues, cells) change in the course of time, but the *form* does not. *Form*, the generative principle of the successive states of my being, may be defined as the spiritual DNA that warrants my unicity and continuity while everything in my body is transformed. This is the interesting thesis of Hillman.

I see things in a different way; the elusive thing that Hillman names *character* does not define for me the existential consistency and continuity of a person but rather its being in the eyes of the others. The continuity of my being is not in my body or in my character; it is in the perception that other persons have of my changing body and of my changing linguistic interactions.

The relation to the sphere of the other is in my view what defines the ever-changing self. The continuity of our being, the continuity of the existential flow, stands out on the background of the gaze of the self as other. I am other for me, inasmuch as I'm witnessing my own becoming, I'm consciously traversing my adventures; I'm suffering from what is happening to my body and my soul.

Our body is a stranger to us – the bodily self is independent from the conscious self. Between these two selves a complex dynamic exists: self-perception.

The continuity of experience is the opposite of identity; it is the becoming of my body and of my relation to the other. I perceive the continuity of my being in the becoming of the gaze of the other, and first of all in the gaze of me as another. Because the body is a stranger, and I am another. I 'is' another (*Je est un autre*), for my conscious perception. Actually, what I perceive of my body is the continuous loss of definition of my body itself. Self-perception is the unconscious imagination of my becoming, of the decomposition and final dissolution of my self.

This exteriority of the self to corporeality, this looking at the body from outside, is the ever-changing feature of (dis) identity. Pleasure and embarrassment, a sense of inadequacy and the uncountable nuances of bodily self-perception accompany human existence from the beginning to the end – but ageing emphasises this unfamiliarity, this painful exteriority, this incongruousness of the bodily self that changes, and resists change, and finally betrays me.

Growing old essentially means the continuous degrading of self-perception. Self-perception is the perception of a radical alterity, an experience of the unidentical self, as it ceaselessly eludes identity.

Growing old implies the enhancement of this consciousness of nonidentity: the other that my body is in relation to
me is less and less responsive, less and less compliant with the
expectations that I have about myself. Less and less able to
automatically reply to stimulations. This is why growing old
implies the most radical reflection on the bodily self.

The matter that the unconscious is made of does not belong
to us, as we cannot master the dynamics of that psychic stuff.
Corporeality also becomes a foreign land as it loses the lightness of the young body, and it becomes a site of heaviness,
ineptness, pain.

But the elusive and uncanny rules that Freud invented for
the elaboration of the Unconscious do not apply. Certainly the
body has its own semiotics, and doctors are the interpreters
of physical symptoms, but the psychoanalytic interpretation is
interpretation of signs of language, not of the gradual degrading of tissues, of cells and of the brain.

Growing old implies a loss of definition in a neurophysi-
ological sense: the tissues that process perceptual information,
the mucosa that softens the contact with the other are losing
their flexibility, their precision, their refinement. This loss
triggers an alteration of the relation to others, of the relation
between perception and language.

When the organism grows old and its tissues stiffen, the
individual gradually tends to reduce the superfluous acts, the
nervous investments that are not directly aimed at survival.
This is why motion becomes heavy, and slow and rigid. No
more the elegant dance of courtesy, but the rational pursuing
of the goal with the minimal effort.

In my old age I have learned to reduce to a minimum the
displacements of my body in the room in which I dwell. This
removal of the superfluous brings about a painful impoverishment of experience: let's think of courtesy, to the courteous
elaboration of the relation with the other. Courtesy implies
first of all the ability to interpret quite subtle nonverbal

signals, sometime unintentional or unconscious: sensibility. Furthermore, courtesy implies the investment of psychological (and also physical) energy, movements of the hands and of the gaze, special dispositions of the utterance and so on: all things that have no immediate useful function.

This is why old people are often cantankerous, bad tempered, malicious: they cannot waste their residual energy in the aesthetic elaboration of behaviour, enunciation, physical movement. No more dance, no more courteous inflexion, no more courting: the communication of the senescent organism tends to the essential, to mere survival and effectiveness.

14

Pleasure and Desire

It is hard to contend against desire, because it takes what it craves from our soul.

Heraclitus

Ever since Eros became separated from Logos and opposed to it, and ever since historical rationality has been conceived as a separate sphere, unrelated to erotic desire, history has been dominated by the economic principle. This principle reduces other bodies to instruments of accumulation instead of partners in pleasure.

We need to analyse in depth the reasons for this separation and for the devaluation of the body that results from it. The opposition between Eros and Logos originates in the distinction between eros and agape, between ethical and erotic love. This is the origin of the historical impracticability of love and the confinement of equality into the space of utopia. But what do we mean by *love*? The word, intrinsically linked to the message of Jesus Christ, acquires all its social power during the Romantic age and finally becomes a mere advertising gadget in late modernity, when any residual human dignity has been degraded to commodity status.

Are we to understand love as eros or agape? As desire or as friendship?

Let us abandon the word *love*, which is too overloaded with meaning to still really mean anything, and focus instead on two more specific concepts that the philosophical and psychoanalytic traditions have distinguished and even opposed: desire and pleasure.

We know that desire is creative tension, while pleasure is the release of that tension, and thus a moment of harmony between the body and its environment. *Creative tension* means that the object of desire does not precede desire but is a projection of desire itself. Obviously, the desired persons have their own separate lives, but you don't desire them in their separateness – you desire the situation that your imagination creates in your relation with them.

In Plato's *Symposium*, Aristophanes says that eroticism is the aspiration to recompose the original unity of the human being. At the dawn of human adventure there were androgynes who had two faces, four arms, four legs and two sexes. Zeus, fearing the power of their self-sufficiency, cut them in half. From that traumatic act was born the human species as we know it. Love, then, is our nostalgia for our old completeness, and desire is the tension towards rejoining our lost half. Pleasure, on the other hand, consists in the temporary reconstitution of the original androgyne.

Then comes Agathon, who speaks after Aristophanes. He is a beautiful young poet who reads his poems in the city's theatres. Agathon begins his talk with a distinction between Eros and its effects. Eros, he argues, is the incarnation of beauty, but its effects on the human being are painful, because more than anything else, desire is a lack and a tension that can never be satisfied.

Then it is Socrates's turn, and he refers to what Diotima taught him: love is the desire for a gradual ascent that at first encounters erotic bodies, then noble souls and finally beauty as supreme value. The love that Diotima taught him, says Socrates – anticipating an idea that will come back in Christianity with the early Renaissance poets – is the path that guides the human being to perfection and wisdom.

At that point, the young Alcibiades arrives, a little elated and drunk. He reproaches Socrates for refusing to make love to him, even though he's beautiful and desired by all the young women of Athens. In Alcibiades's words surfaces the idea that knowledge comes from direct contact, a theme found in another Platonic or pseudo-Platonic dialogue, the *Theages*. In this dialogue, attributed to Plato (but probably spurious), a former student tells Socrates that being next to him, physically touching and being touched by him, made him grow in wisdom, as if carnal conjunction allowed knowledge to be transferred between two bodies:

> 'I will tell you, Socrates,' he said, 'what is incredible, upon my soul, yet true. For I never yet learnt anything from you, as you know yourself: but I made progress, whenever I was with you, if I was merely in the same house, without being in the same room, but more progress, when I was in the same room. And it seemed to me to be much more when I was in the same room and looked at you as you were speaking, than when I turned my eyes elsewhere: but my progress was by far the greatest and most marked whenever I sat beside you and held and touched you.'[1]

That implies that the sensuous exchange between bodies is the condition of knowledge, and in particular of ethical knowledge, which has nothing to do with the law, the rules or the moral values, but is the knowledge of the pleasure of the other, and our sensitivity to it.

Unfortunately, however, in our postmodern times ethics has drowned in an ocean of shit: our relation with the other has been reduced to competition with an Other that has become disembodied.

The nexus between desire and pleasure is the energy that makes ethical knowledge and courtesy possible. It is a game based on language and caresses.

In a book that I found enlightening, *Sul piacere che manca* (The missing pleasure, 2019), Paolo Godani quotes a letter written by Gilles Deleuze speaking about his relationship with Foucault:

'The last time we met, Michel, very gently and with true affection, said to me something like this: I can't stand the word desire ... and he added: maybe I call pleasure what you call desire, but in any case I need another word.'[2]

Here I'll do an autobiographical detour, which is also a self-critique. I adhered to the thought of Deleuze and Guattari in 1976, while I was in jail and a friend sent me a copy of their first common book, *Anti-Oedipus*. But since the very beginning, I ignored the difference between pleasure and desire, and now I understand that this was a serious omission.

Maybe because I lived a life of pleasure (except when I was in jail), I never thought about pleasure, and my philosophical spin was centred on the concept of desire.

But now it is time to make amends: maybe because in my old age pleasure has become hardly attainable while desire torments me, I have finally understood the difference between the two concepts, which in the past seemed irrelevant to me. Desire is the tension that pushes us towards an object that does not exist, but that we create in that movement. Far from being the fulfillment of a need, or the remedy of a lack, desire is the creation of the other as attractor and myth.

Desire is king in the realm of the imagination, and this is why the forces pervading the social sphere are born and organised in the domain of desire. This is the message of *Anti-Oedipus*, a book that had decisive influence on not only my own thought but also the thought of an entire generation of autonomous rebels at the end of the 1970s, when social movements escaped the economic reduction and integrated the unconscious dimension in all processes of social subjectivation.

We thought that if desire is the strongest attractor – actually an irresistible one as Heraclitus suggests in his fragment I previously quoted – in the relation between sensible and conscious beings and builds the most radical bonds, then the only way to finally make history a human dimension where happiness and peace are possible was to build an alliance between eros and agape, desire and friendship.

The message of love, which in the Christian faith had a sacrificial aspect, seemed to have found a materialistic foundation in the concept of desire and in the experience of anti-authoritarian movements based on desire.

'Happiness is subversive when it becomes collective,' said one of the slogans of the 'desiring autonomy' movement (*autonomia desiderante*): this meant that joy is a feeling that can be purely individual but acquires a political power if it spreads to the social environment. And it also implies that you cannot be happy if you are surrounded by flows of suffering and depression.

But the exclusive emphasis on desire coming from our reading of the works of Deleuze and Guattari eventually caused a nervous breakdown of our collective energies, a breakdown that Jean Baudrillard had repeatedly addressed (never explicitly, never rudely) in his critique of Deleuzian-Guattarian thought.

But now that pleasure is failing me (besides the pleasure of reading *Sul piacere che manca* by Godani). I realise that without a symbiosis with pleasure, desire turns into the cruel motor of an endless and joyless race: the psychological engine of capitalism, as Baudrillard used to say.

Desire belongs to the imagination, while pleasure belongs to the real.

Capitalism, and the increasingly ferocious and accelerated networks of semiocapitalism, act as constant mobilisations of desire and infinite interdictions of pleasure. An economy of accumulation pushes you to desire, but it interdicts pleasure, and above all cancels the very time for pleasure, because all your time must be spent on competing, on accumulating, and thus on desiring, virtually and endlessly.

This raises the question of the relation between desire and death that Freud had already posed in his own way.

Godani says, 'If we don't want to reintroduce the death drive, we need to recognise that there are deadly effects that don't originate in a fundamental drive, but in the dynamics of desire … What exists is not the desire for death, but the deadly effects of desire.'[3]

Capitalism incessantly produces its deadly effects not via an original death drive but from the psychological dynamics of a competitive economy. If desire is tension, projection and impulse, then pleasure is the harmony between a singular sensual drift and the rhythm of the cosmos, the fusion of the vibration of two different bodies.

In other words, as Godani says, 'The flesh of pleasure is always *gratiae plena*. The cosmic condition of grace does not come suddenly, but constitutes its only mode of appearance.'[4]

Grace is the suspension of the weight of being, and a desire that does not include the possibility of pleasure is graceless – it torments the soul and causes suffering.

15

Exhaustion

The Cultural Construction of 'Future'

At the end of the acceleration cycle, extinction looms.

Beyond the pandemic threshold we enter a period of exhaustion: not only have our physical energies been drained by the virus, but nervous energy has waned, abruptly breaking the rhythm of social mobilisation. At the economic level the demand is in free fall not only because consumers are forced to stay home but also because of the deflation of consumerist excitement. This collective excitement has deteriorated, and this is not merely an economic deflation; it is the cause of the persistent economic downturn. The recession is the outcome of a psychological disinvestment, the consequence of a widespread withdrawal of desire.

This downturn brings about a conceptual reconfiguration of the very concept of Future: first of all we should disentangle the concept of *future* (and also the psychological tension towards *future*) from the expectations of growth, expansion and acceleration, which shaped the concept of future in modern culture and imagination.

Although the widespread consciousness and perception of this deflation of future is an effect of the abrupt interruption provoked by the lockdown, we should not forget that deflation was already underway. For at least two decades before the pandemic, the fact that expansion was nearing its end for non-economic reasons (environment, mental suffering) was obvious to every thinking person on the planet, with the noticeable exception of economists.

Expansion grows impossible when the physical limits of the world and the neurological limits of the brain have been reached. Since that point on, the acceleration of the rhythm of communication and life has a destructive effect on the social mind, as the nervous system is disturbed by permanent hyperstimulation. The neoliberal cycle, which lasted around four decades, was essentially an attempt in postponing the big psycho-deflation and deferring the economic stagnation by the acceleration of mental productivity (nervous exploitation) and the devaluation of physical productivity (low salaries, precariousness).

Extractivism of the physical resources of the planet and of the nervous resources of the brain has been the neoliberal reaction to the tendential fall in the rate of profit, but it has rapidly brought about the exhaustion of physical and nervous resources.

The virus obliged the reluctant authorities of the world to accept the evidence: the age of expansion is over. They do not dare to recognise this *apertis verbis*, of course. But they are paralysed, or panicking, as the truth has been exposed: capitalism is dead.

Now our cultural task is to think future out of the conceptual framework of expansion. Decoupling the concept of future from the expectation of expansion and acceleration means getting free from the framework of capitalism. But the separation of production from accumulation, of the useful from exchange value, of pleasure from consumption is unthinkable.

Escaping from the capitalist frame implies the reactivation of a social energy of solidarity that seems unachievable after forty years of neoliberal reform and of connective mutation.

Since the triumph of neoliberalism we have been taught that there is no alternative to capitalism, capitalism being the economic and cultural insurmountable border of human history. Now it's crystal clear: if this neoliberal assumption is true, then we have to resign ourselves to the idea that extinction is the only future that our progeny can expect.

However, I think that the neoliberal assumption is not true, and an alternative does exist: it is based on liberation from the obsession of economic growth; it is based on the redistribution of resources, on the reduction of labour time, and on the expansion of time dedicated to the free activity of teaching, researching, healing and taking care.

Establishing usefulness (not accumulation of value) as the criterion for social production is the alternative to the idolatry of the market, to the obsession with profit. This alternative is based only on a psychocultural conversion to frugality and friendship. It is hard to tell if, beyond the pandemic threshold, frugality and friendship will prevail. At present it is not evident. Much will depend on the readjustment of the social Unconscious; much will depend on the cultural ability to withdraw from the instinct of accumulation, which is not an instinct indeed, but a cultural construct. Much will depend on the cultural ability to reframe the perception of future.

Modern culture, and particularly modern aesthetics, deeply internalised the identification of future and expansion. The futurist movement sprung up in the two most backward countries of the European continent – namely Italy and Russia – as the harbinger of expansion, acceleration and subjugation of nature as marks of the desired Future.

Italian futurism, in fact, was particularly conscious of the aggressive implications of this aesthetic. In the *Manifesto del futurismo*, published in 1909, Filippo Tommaso Marinetti and his pals proclaimed that acceleration is a path to potency: military potency and economic potency are based on the speed of the machines, as Paul Virilio has explained in his studies on dromocracy (the power of speed), which present military supremacy from the point of view of military velocity.

Acceleration and Impotence

Now in this new century we are miles away from that world of a masculine youthful sentiment of expansion and potency, and the virus has exposed our impotence with an unprecedented explicitness.

The hyperacceleration that digital technology has imposed upon the world in the last few decades has provoked an effect of exhaustion: physical, psychological and mental. At the same time the demographical trends of the Northern Hemisphere of planet Earth point to a rapid process of senescence of the population.

The more the digital machine is powerful and fast, the less humans can rationally decipher and politically govern their environment, and the more impotent they feel.

In *Die Antiquiertheit des Menschen*, Günther Anders writes about the humiliation that is implicit in the confrontation of men with their own automatic creatures, and he announces that in this kind of humiliation there are the seeds of the *Übermensch* returning in all his fury.

Nazism, according to Anders, is not to be remembered as a bad memory of the past but has to be considered as a nightmare ready for the future. In his appalling prediction, future Nazism will be the effect of the humiliation of humans overwhelmed by the enormity of their own products that are ruled by forces of economic automatism and subtracted from conscious control.

The Anders prediction comes true with the rise of worldwide Trumpism, when the humiliated get their revenge by destroying the Reason embodied in the algorithmic machine. But the humiliation has been intensified during the months of the lockdown, when billions of humans have been obliged to hide in order to escape the overpowering invisible force of the virus.

This is where we are now: the wave of dementia that has been overwhelming the world since the year 2016, which erupted with Brexit and the victory of Trump, can be read, in my opinion, as a sort of furious reaction to the invincible power of the techno-linguistic automatisms embedded in the financial machine. What now? What will be the reaction of the social psyche to a new overpowering force which is more pervasive and more frightening than finance: the unconscious force of contagion?

Will we at last be able to face reality, to renounce to the presumption of human omnipotence? Will we finally accept the idea that we are part of a system of reciprocity, of mutual interaction? Will we accept the idea that we are mortal? This is the point: facing mortality, and abandoning the obsession of total control.

The crucial point here is the relation between reason and chaos. The modern project was based on the dubious assumption that the infinite complexity of the universe can be reduced to rational knowledge expressed in mathematical terms and therefore can be submitted to political control. That project has been enormously productive, enriching and progressive, up to a certain point. Then the extreme complication of the social exceeded the sphere of scientific knowledge and rational control. At that point complexity grew into chaos, and political reason was confronted by its limits.

The intrinsic madness of capitalism was exposed at that point: capitalism cannot exist without a never-ending strain of accumulation, acceleration and expansion, so that the collective brain is engaged in a struggle against chaos, aimed at dominating chaos and submitting chaos to the principle of valorisation.

But remember: those who wage war against chaos will be defeated, as chaos feeds upon war. Therefore capitalism slammed against the impenetrable wall of Chaos, and social life crashed as a result.

The virus reminded us of our limits and obliged a slow-down that is not a provisional pause but the arrival point of the modern race. Now we are facing the alternative between reframing the expectations of future or paving the way to extinction.

Historically fascism (in all its different forms, including the Stakhanovist cult of industrialisation) was the cultural push towards full modernity, an impetus towards the intensification of productivity, consumption, information. In the new century the fascist mythology has returned, mixing together nationalism, racism and sheer ignorance. But the essential potency of twentieth-century fascism has not returned, because it was based on something that now is no more: the expansive force of industrial capitalism and the expansive violence of colonialism.

Despite the many analogies with the old fascist movement, the spreading dementia of Trumpism is decisively different on this crucial point: the fascist movement of a hundred years ago was based on the enthusiastic expectation of a future of expansion, of colonial conquest and glory and increasing prosperity. The young men of Italy, Germany and Japan were reclaiming their right to take part in the imperialist colonisation of the world, and the increasing productivity of the economy authorised their optimism and their trust in the future.

The horizon today looks quite different: not the youngish aggressive euphoria of the futurists, but the looming depression of the precarious generation. Not the push to colonise Southern countries, not the glorification of the act of invasion and occupation as an act of civilisation, but the fear of a massive counterinvasion and the ensuing rejection of migrants who today come from countries that have been plundered by the white colonisers.

Despite its violence, fascism was part of the push towards industrial progress, so it could depict itself as an act of civilisation.

The present suprematism is essentially a defensive phenomenon intended to reassert a declining privilege of the white Western people. The so-called populist movements have little to do with the colonialist aggressiveness of the past, which was led by the ideological expectation of an improvement of life.

Forty years of financial violence and social humiliation have transformed the majority of white populations to the point that they are now psychopathically aggressive and impervious to human sensibility. The new reactionary movement that is spreading worldwide is not ideological but cynical and somehow suicidal.

Death Instinct

Why has capitalism grown so aggressive, so selfish and at the end so destructive, why have the old days of the reasonable industrial bourgeoisie turned, why is the new capitalist class so cruel? There are cultural reasons for this metamorphosis of the proprietary class, and there are also material reasons.

The old bourgeoisie was a strongly territorialised class and was conscious that profit and social welfare have to go more or less together: the prosperity of the bourgeoisie could not be dissociated or opposed to the increase of social demand and to the relative welfare of the community in which the bourgeois was dwelling.

In the last part of the twentieth century the globalisation of the capitalist cycle had totally severed the links between capital and territory: the margins for profit and capital accumulation have been narrowing after the stagflation of the 1970s and have been narrowing again in the first two decades of the new century as a consequence of technological automation. The long-lasting lockdown of 2020 and 2021 is provoking a catastrophic reduction in the margins for profit. Therefore we have to expect an increased ferocity of financial capitalism.

Contrary to the old industrial bourgeoisie, which drew its economic power from the welfare of society, the global financial class has never been interested in the welfare of the community, as it could make profits only by destroying that welfare and extracting value from the destruction of public services. Globalisation has destroyed the national protections of the worker class, thus setting into motion a race for the plundering of the exhausted resources of the earth.

Three irreversible phenomena of late modernity led expansion to a halt:

First, the plundering and ensuing exhaustion of the physical resources that enabled industrialisation and urbanisation in the past (water, breathable air, oil and so on).

Second, the exploitation of the nervous resources of societies, leading them to collapse.

Third, the ageing populations of the global North, the ageing and senescence of the global brain, and the following loss of perceptions of future.

Senectus mundi: the ageing of the world is the result of a demographic trend and the prolonging of lifetimes and simultaneous downturn of birth rates in the North. But it is also an effect of the social perception that economic growth has reached its limit.

Because of its futuristic imprint, the political mind is unable to assimilate and elaborate the exhaustion and the end of growth – so politicians have been insisting on the legitimacy of expansionist rhetoric based on the failing promise of recovery, and of growth. But this kind of late futurism now is a dangerous instinct, one that is leading to collapse: the collapse arrived in the spring of 2020, after the worldwide convulsion that in the autumn of 2019 shook the world, from Hong Kong to Santiago de Chile, from Paris to Quito, to Beirut to Tehran, in a violent inconclusive attempt to subvert the established powers.

End of Growth

The notion of growth is crucial to the conceptual construction of modern economics, so the policies of all the governments in the world are based on the assumption that only growth is good, while frugality and redistribution are bad.

When social production happens not to comply with economic expectations of growth, economists decree that society is sick, and they name this disease by the frightening word: *recession*. This diagnosis has nothing to do with the needs of populations, because it does not refer to the use value of things and of semiotic goods but to abstract capitalist accumulation, which is an accumulation of exchange value.

Growth, in the economic sense, is not about the increase of social happiness or the satisfaction of the basic needs of people; it is about the expansion of financial profits and the expansion of the global volume of exchange value. Gross national product – the main indicator of growth – is not a measure of social welfare and pleasure, but a monetary measure.

Social happiness or unhappiness generally do not depend on the amount of money circulating in the economy; rather they depend on the distribution of wealth and in the balance of cultural expectations and availability of physical and semiotic goods.

Much more than an economic criterion of the evaluation of social well-being, growth is a confirmation of the expectation of the future as infinite expansion.

In the years following the financial crash of 2008, the Harvard economist Lawrence Summers, among others, has repeatedly pronounced the words *secular stagnation*.

The first cause of the stagnation is that, according to Summers, 'in a period of rapid technological change, it can make sense to defer investment lest new technology soon make the old obsolete'.[1]

Actually, the relative decline in demand has various causes:

those who have purchase power don't need to spend, and those who need to acquire things have no money. The more inequality rises, the more the economy is doomed to stagnate.

In such a situation the only way to achieve growth (in purely monetary terms) is to financially plunder the declining resources of society and to destroy the wealth that was built in the industrial past: the dismissal of infrastructures and the dismantlement of public education, public health and public transportation. In short, the only way to counter secular stagnation is by destroying society in order to support profit and financial accumulation.

Here we find the most important contradiction of contemporary capitalism: while new technologies have enormously enhanced the productivity of labour, this improvement has paradoxically provoked an impoverishment of workers and of society at large. The effect of technology is that less labour is needed, so the only solution would be a reduction of work time without reduction of wages. But this is unthinkable inside the neoliberal framework, so an opportunity is turned into a damnation. Wages go down, economic demand languishes, deflation takes the place of inflation, and depression looms at the horizon. The creation of a semiocapitalist sphere opened a new possibility to expansion, and for some years in the 1990s the economy could euphorically expand, and the net economy was expected to create a new prospect of infinite growth. But in the long run this was a deception, because, even if the general intellect is infinitely productive, the limits to growth are inscribed in the affective body of the cognitive labourer: they are limits of attention, of psychic energy, limits of a suffering sensibility.

After the delusions of the new economy – diffused by the wired neoliberal ideologists at the end of the past century – came the deception of the dot-com crash, announcing, at the very beginning of the new century, the coming collapse of the financial economy. Since September 2008 we know that, notwithstanding the financial virtualisation of expansion, growth is no longer an increase of wealth but only an increase in abstract value.

Then came the virus, and concreteness returned: the virus is a concrete particle of matter that jeopardises the relation between economy and life.

Now it's clear that the identification of the future with growth is leading us to extinction. Only by decoupling the future from expansion and acceleration, only by accepting the message of the virus can we survive. The virus's message is that expansion is over, and exhaustion is the overall trend.

Defying both optimistic and apocalyptic visions of the future in her cryptic way, Donna Haraway speaks of the looming extinction in terms that are simultaneously dreadful and unwinding, tragic and ironic:

> [I'm] especially impatient with two responses that I hear all too frequently to the horrors of the Anthropocene and the Capitalocene. The first is easy to describe and, I think, dismiss, namely, a comic faith in technofixes, whether secular or religious: technology will somehow come to the rescue of its naughty but very clever children, or what amounts to the same thing, God will come to the rescue of his disobedient but ever hopeful children. In the face of such touching silliness about technofixes (or techno-apocalypses), sometimes it is hard to remember that it remains important to embrace situated technical projects and their people. They are not the enemy; they can do many important things for staying with the trouble and for making generative oddkin.
>
> The second response, harder to dismiss, is probably even more destructive: namely, a position that the game is over, it's too late, there's no sense trying to make anything any better, or at least no sense having any active trust in each other in working and playing for a resurgent world. Some scientists I know express this kind of bitter cynicism, even as they actually

work very hard to make a positive difference for both people and other critters. Some people who describe themselves as critical cultural theorists or political progressives express these ideas too. I think the odd coupling of actually working and playing for multispecies flourishing with tenacious energy and skill, while expressing an explicit 'game over' attitude that can and does discourage others, including students, is facilitated by various kinds of futurisms. One kind seems to imagine that only if things work do they matter – or, worse, only if what I and my fellow experts do works to fix things does anything matter. More generously, sometimes scientists and others who think, read, study, agitate, and care know too much, and it is too heavy. Or, at least we think we know enough to reach the conclusion that life on earth that includes human people in any tolerable way really is over, that the apocalypse really is nigh.

That attitude makes a great deal of sense in the midst of the earth's sixth great extinction event and in the midst of engulfing wars, extractions, and immiserations of billions of people and other critters for something called 'profit' or 'power' – or, for that matter, called 'God'. A game-over attitude imposes itself in the gale-force winds of feeling, not just knowing, that human numbers are almost certain to reach more than 11 billion people by 2100. This figure represents a 9-billion-person increase over 150 years from 1950 to 2100, with vastly unequal consequences for the poor and the rich – not to mention vastly unequal burdens imposed on the earth by the rich compared to the poor – and even worse consequences for nonhumans almost everywhere. There are many other examples of dire realities; the Great Accelerations of the post–World War II era gouge their marks in earth's rocks, waters, airs, and critters. There is a fine line between acknowledging the extent and seriousness of the troubles and succumbing to abstract futurism and its affects of sublime despair and its politics of sublime indifference.[2]

Let's stop expecting salvation from technology; let's stop expecting apocalypse from technology. Extinction is certain if the demographic trend is confirmed, if we don't find a way to escape the double challenge of hyperpopulation and senility. The combination of a global demographic explosion and ageing Northern population will result in simultaneous depression and despairing aggressiveness. The escape rope can't be found in the kingdom of political will or that of rational government. Only a cultural and psychological inversion of the self-defeating expectations of growth may defuse the bomb. Only the abandonment (highly unlikely at the present) of the obsession of identity may defuse the bomb.

Children

The words that Greta Thunberg uttered on 22 September 2019 at the United Nations marked a turning point:

> You have stolen my dreams and my childhood with your empty words. And yet I'm one of the lucky ones. People are suffering. People are dying. Entire ecosystems are collapsing. We are in the beginning of a mass extinction. And all you can talk about is money and fairy tales of eternal economic growth. How dare you![3]

These words are not only a reproach against the inept and arrogant global political class; they're also a decrial of economic obsessions. Reading Greta's denouncement of the fairy tales of eternal economic growth, I realise that the millennial generation is facing the same enemy that my generation was facing fifty years ago: capitalism, the fanatic obsession of growth, accumulation and profit.

These fifty years have passed in vain, probably because my generation has been paralysed by a political superstition: my generation has been paralysed by the superstitious belief that political will can master the infinite complexity of the world social becoming. Five decades of struggles, of delusions and of defeats, have finally proved that political will is impotent, unfit and unable to govern the intricacy of economic interests, religious prejudices, selfishness, ignorance and, most of all, the cultural instinct that identifies the future with expansion.

I don't know if the new movement rebelling against a man-made extinction will be able to stop the deadly effects of the Capitalocene, and I don't know if this generation will be able to revert the effects of extractivist aggressiveness, raging ethnonationalism, military power and wars.

What I expect, however, is a cultural transformation of expectations, lifestyles and psychological investments. Not a political change – that means little at this point – but a change in daily life: this may be the result of the widespread Fridays for Future movement that is marching in the cities of the world.

'Our house is on fire' is the slogan uttered by the activists of Extinction Rebellion. However, in a speech at the London Climate Strike on 20 September 2019, the Wretched of the Earth coalition replied:

Our house has been on fire for over 500 years.

And it did not set itself on fire.

We did not get here by a sequence of small missteps and mistakes.

We were thrust here by powerful forces that drove the unequal distribution of resources and the rigged structure of our societies.

The economic system that dominates us was brought about by colonial projects whose sole purpose is the pursuit of domination and profit.

For centuries, racism, sexism and classism have been necessary for this system to be upheld, and have shaped the conditions we find ourselves in.[4]

This implies that a greener economy in the countries of Europe will achieve very little if they continue to hinder countries in the Global South from doing the same through crippling debt, unfair trade deals and the export of their own deadly extractive industries. The hyperdeveloped countries have been producing the conditions of the impending climate crisis, so they cannot escape their responsibility – they cannot refuse to pay a fair share in dealing with it.

It is impossible to separate climate justice from a worldwide program of redistribution of wealth and resources.

When we speak of the prospect of extinction, we are not speaking just of climate change and devastation of the physical environment of the planet; we are speaking also of the legacy of five centuries of colonialism and the exploitation of the nervous resources of human beings. We are speaking of social inequality, massive displacement of people trapped by war and misery, the rejection and marginalisation of migrants, and the inhuman detention of millions of migrants in concentration camps that surround the developed countries, in the Mediterranean Basin, at the Mexican border, and in many other places in the world.

Directed by the Lebanese filmmaker Nadine Labaki, the film *Capernaum* tells the story of undocumented refugees and migrants in Beirut from the perspective of children who don't understand why they are born into poverty, displaced by war, neglected and mistreated. In interviews about the film, Labaki has said that when you ask those children whether they are glad they were born, they answer they are not and wonder why they were born at all. The premise of the story is a young Lebanese boy who takes legal action against his parents for giving birth to him. But as Labaki says in an interview with the *New York Times*, 'He's actually not only suing his parents, he's suing the whole system because his parents are also victims of that system – one that is failing on so many levels and that completely ends up excluding people.'[5]

This is the other face of the rallying call of Greta Thunberg, and it is no less significant from a cultural and political point of view. Northern kids are feeling the heat of climate change, but Southern kids are feeling hunger, misery and terror: so the old punk provocation 'no future' is turning into a sort of common sense at the beginning of the third millennium.

16

The American Insurrection as Preventive Psychotherapy

Stay together, stay tight.
We do this every night!

Slogan of Portland activists

When I wrote that the pandemic environment (lockdown, social distancing, phobic sensibilisation) is the best cultural soup for a wave of autism, I was not strictly referring to a psychopathology but to a psychocultural trend: the impending psycho-scape is marked by the possibility of a widespread diffusion of desensibilisation to the other.

When reasoning about the collective psycho-sphere, we should avoid generalisations, and most of all we should avoid being deterministic. I'm not saying people will be 'phobically sensibilised'; I'm saying that the spectrum of mental disease will lean towards a phobic sensibilisation.

Psychoanalysts, no less than activists and artists, should focus on this perspective. Psychoanalysts should elaborate a therapeutic methodology for avoiding a pandemic of regression, autism and depression.

I'll try now to be more clear on this point.

In the weeks that followed the murder of George Floyd, an insurrection exploded in American cities. The political message of that insurrection is crystal clear: We, Black people, Latinos and precarious workers, have been the main target of the virus because we have limited access to the expensive health system and are victims of the racism embedded in American culture and of the systematic violence of police. We have said many times with James Baldwin, 'The fire next time!' Now it is next time, and we'll reply with fire to the fire.

But the American insurrection has not only a political significance. In my opinion it has also a psychotherapeutic implication.

According to the *Guardian*, 'those aged under twenty-five are three times more likely to report that they are not enjoying their day-to-day activities as much as they were two years ago, while almost half said they were struggling to concentrate, compared with just over a fifth in 2018'.[1]

Certainly the economic effect of the pandemic is going to be especially resented by the new generation whose expectations have been thwarted so early.

'The research revealed that a third of this age group had lost their job in the pandemic, compared with one sixth of working-age adults generally, and that those currently on furlough expect to have an increased risk of later unemployment when the job retention scheme ends.'[2]

But the psychological effect of the contagion is no less important, because it is directly affecting the process of social subjectivation, solidarity, autonomy and joy.

Can we imagine a political strategy, and a psychotherapeutic strategy, to heal suffering subjectivity? Democratic participation is a deceit, as politics is clearly unable to keep any promise, and democracy is empty, boring and fake. I think that repressed energy has to erupt freely, and that the fear of death has to be overcome: insurrection is the only way to heal the suffering of millions. The American insurrection that exploded after the execution of George Floyd is the proof of this.

After the long-lasting lockdowns of 2020 and 2021, after the long-lasting misery and suffering in small uncomfortable houses, after a long period of distancing and loneliness, millions of young Americans have thought more or less, 'Our mental balance is in danger. If we do not react to intolerable acts of violence and humiliation like the atrocious public execution of George Floyd, we are going to enter a tunnel of eternal depression; we will be swamped by a suicidal wave.

'We must react, and we have to do it now, even if it is going to be dangerous because the pandemic is still here, and because the police are no less murderous than the coronavirus. It will be dangerous, but we must react now.'

So they got out in the streets, they marched, they chanted, but also they attacked and burned the buildings of the police; they also looted stores and supermarkets; they launched Molotov cocktails; they responded with fire to the fire of the racists. They paid a high price: Young activists have been killed by police and white supremacists. Thousands of them have been arrested. But dying is not the worst thing that can happen, when the prospect is to survive amid racism, misery, unemployment, the virus and the police.

But the stakes are not only political: the humiliation that racists are imposing on us is not only dangerous for our physical survival; it is dangerous too for our psychological condition, for our dignity (whatever the word *dignity* means), for our possibility of enjoying life.

Therefore we must say loud and clear: We are no more ready to exchange our survival with systematic humiliation. We are ready to fight and to die, because dying is not the worst future for those who are young in these times.

If you focus on eroticism and sociability, you understand that a huge catastrophe is underway. For the first time in history the physical proximity of bodies is in danger, and the approaching of lips is abhorrent. Potentially this is a nuclear bomb upon social solidarity. Solidarity means nothing if it is not based on the pleasure of the presence of the other. Solidarity is not a moral concept; it is an affective one.

What about solidarity if we'll be led to suspect, to fear, to avoid the presence of the body of the other?

The young Americans' insurrection paves a possible pathway of emancipation from the depressive backlash of the pandemic. I see this insurrection as a psychotherapeutic explosion, one that risked creating a surge in the contagion, and risked provoking greater repression (10,000 people were placed under arrest in the first month after Floyd's execution). These are danger signals, but the insurrection paid dividends in terms of psychic healing and social solidarity.

The uprising has shown a possible way out from the protracted lockdown and a form of respiration for a society that is suffocating. Permanent insurrection is the only way to breathe, the only way to avoid a deep psychological depression in the coming months and years.

During the lockdown, young Americans – and not only Americans – have been experiencing loneliness, fear, powerlessness and mostly suffocation.

Panic crises have quadrupled.[3]

Friends who work in mental health centres say that there is a surge in suicide, particularly among young people.

How can we emerge from this claustrophobia? The uprising is exposing young people to the virus, that's true. But inaction would expose them to a tunnel of depression and suicidal drive in the next future. The American insurrection is an answer to this dilemma. Only insurrection can save us from a long-lasting depression: insurrection means togetherness, solidarity, embrace, friendship, mutual assistance, erotic pleasure, collective orgasm, exorcism.

I don't know if the American upheaval is the beginning of a world cycle – I hope so. There will be no economic recovery in the next few years, because economic growth is over, debt is exploding, and insolvency will spread unavoidably. We must turn insolvency into a conscious, intentional, political act of refusal, of self-organisation, an act of rejection of monetary alienation.

This situation will be extremely volatile, and social subjectivity may veer unpredictably. The only way to escape the dire psychological consequences of this catastrophe is social autonomy, economic egalitarianism and a common act of rebellion.

I use the word *uprising*, but I am not referring to the experiences of armed struggles of the past. The Black Panthers belong to the landscape of the 1960s and '70s, and their armed experience cannot be proposed again, because the disproportion between the movement and the imperialist state is so enormous that thinking of an armed struggle would be suicidal.

The spirit of the Black Panthers, of the Red Brigades and of the Rote Armee Fraktion is out of the picture. However, misery, exploitation, police violence, racism have persisted and worsened in the last decades.

The force of the movement has changed ground: we do not need guns, because cognitive workers have weapons much more explosive and annihilating than guns. We should deploy the force of techno-cultural sabotage, and the force of techno-scientific invention, in order to fight for our well-being and also in order to reprogram from scratch the social machine.

We should avoid the repetition of the old antifascist discourse, which was based on the goal of the Restoration of Democracy. We should avoid this trap, because democracy is dead and is no more appealing. The root of suffering is not fascism, but capitalism. Fascism is essentially a psychotic reaction to impotence and humiliation.

A hundred years ago fascism was the aggressive ideology of a young culture that trusted expansion as economic possibility, as national glory, as individual improvement. Aggressiveness was aimed at expanding the space of white civilisation, of industrial progress. Nothing is left of that landscape: now expansion is over, and economic recovery is an empty promise.

Expansion would mean only further devastation of the physical environment, further devastation of the mental environment.

What we need now is not empty words about democracy, empty words about recovery. Out of the mythology of expansion we have to adopt a frugal, egalitarian culture. Not more useless goods to ingest, but more time to enjoy with our friends, our lovers: this is frugality.

Exhaustion has taken the place of expansion.

Exhaustion, extinction, proximity of death: if we react to this prospect with a reactionary approach aimed at relaunching economic growth at all costs, we will enter a spiral of violence, racism and war. Instead, we must accept the reality of the exhaustion and face reality on egalitarian terms: share frugally what knowledge, solidarity and technology can provide. Redistribution of wealth egalitarianism, frugality: this is the recipe for survival, and possibly for a new pleasurable social life.

According to the sociologist Émile Durkheim, in times of war the suicide rate decreases. People are so busy saving their lives from the bombs, that for a while they forget to kill themselves.

So at the beginning of the quarantine I expected a reduction in the suicide rate, because I equated the quarantine to a war, which was wrong. The psychic effect of the contagion is different from the psycho-effect of war: the main trend is deflation, regression, passivity, while in war you have to be permanently mobilised.

In the second year of the pandemic we don't have final statistics about the suicide rate during the pandemic – we'll have to wait for this. But the accounts of psychologists and psychiatrists speak of a relevant increase in the number of suicides, particularly youngsters.

The immediate causes of this are too easy to detect: you are forbidden to meet your school friends, you are separated from your lover, you feel the shame and the anguish of being a possible bearer of the virus, and so on …

I also think that we are slowly beginning to see the horizon of the century, and we are slowly understanding that extinction is marking that horizon, and we are not prepared to spend our lifetimes under the shadow of the extinction. We must learn to do it, because accepting the horizon of extinction, and avoiding panic, will probably be the only way to escape extinction itself, the only way to find a different horizon, a different future.

Political will has lost autonomy, and most of all it has lost effectiveness because it is subjected to the automatisms of techno-financial capitalism and because it is subjected to the unchaining forces of nature: pandemics, psychosis, climate change …

What is the task of political action in this pandemic time? Enforcing techno-sanitary goals. Those politicians who have rejected the sanitary approach (Trump, Bolsonaro) are the cause of uncountable suffering and death.

They tried to exert the autonomy of political decisions, and the result was catastrophic.

It would be delusional to think that we must seize political power in a revolutionary way or through elections. A revolutionary government would be obliged to bend to the obligations of contagion, of environmental catastrophe, of psychotic explosions.

Human will is impotent: let's accept this reality; let's look for different ways of coming to terms with evolution.

Not political revolution, but schismogenesis – a separation of a part of society from the decaying body of capitalism. Creation and proliferation of autonomous communities, food self-sufficiency, self-defence against police, against the racists and against the state.

This is a strategy for survival and for reinvention, a strategy for healing the psycho-sphere and the social mind.

17

Nothingness – the Alzheimer's of God

Vax Wars

When the virus swiftly spread around the planet we perceived it as a common foe, an invisible common threat, and we felt united as brothers and sisters for a short while.

All of us were united in the fight against nature, which was trying to exterminate us. Human history is an account of a long fight against nature: from this struggle came technology, medicine and complex forms of social organisation.

Then nature began its counterattack, not out of hate for us but as a matter of blind necessity. Abnormal oceanic waves, forest fires, glaciers adrift, the virus.

At first, we felt we were a single body under threat.

Technology came to the rescue, producing the vaccine, a mutagenic prosthesis inserted into the immune system.

Entering the second phase of the Viral Age, however, the prevailing sentiment changed: no longer united by a common threat, people were competing for the life-saving vaccine.

Within months, billions of doses were produced in the Global North, a brand-new supply chain, a new branch of Big Pharma, producing a lifesaver subjected to the rules of intellectual property.

Great Britain, United States, Israel, then continental Europe have launched the race to reach herd immunity. These countries have the money to pay the extortionate demands of Big Pharma.

India and South Africa, both countries ravaged by the contagion, have requested the suspension of intellectual property rights for the vaccines; the World Health Organization has joined in that demand.

No way.

Property rules are much more important than the lives of millions.

By the by, I would say that the CEO and the shareholders of Pfizer or Johnson & Johnson have little or nothing to do with the intellectual process that led to the vaccines' creation of the chemical formula of the vaccine. They know nothing about viruses, chemistry, or bioengineering. They only know how to plunder and accumulate.

In order to save face, the rich countries of Europe and North America promised to be benevolent and send the much-needed vaccines to the countries of the Global South. They created COVAX, which within a year was revealed to be a travesty. As I close this book, in June 2021, only 2 per cent of the African population has received the first dose of a vaccine, while the white race is racing toward herd immunity.

I have expected all along to witness many contradictions arising from the Covid-19 experience. At times, I expected a radical change towards generosity, solidarity, and plane rationality as we struggle with decisions that could determine the survival of our species.

When I realised that the World Trade Organization, the European Union and Big Pharma had decided that proprietary considerations are more important than anything else, including the survival of mankind, I drew a conclusion: the game is over. Human life on the planet is a failed experiment.

The countdown begins.

So, I decided to read Salman Rushdie.

American Quichotte

The baroque and surrealist imagination share a fundamental background: they know that the world is illusion, maya, *artefactum*, a projection of shadows on the screen of the mind.

'They are showing us an endless funky movie in the screen of our brains.' I do not remember if I actually read these words in an interview with Philip K. Dick, or if Philip himself came one night into one of my dreams, whispering those words. I remember that I replied to him, asking, 'They? Who?' Is there some God producing the phantasmagoria that we are experiencing, at a rhythm that permanently accelerates? No, there is no God behind the screen; there are chaotic flows of imagination, technology and language, and these flows disturb the spectrum of consciousness, provoking storms of dementia, fury, depression and despair.

> It was the age of Anything-Can-Happen ... A whole nation might jump off a cliff like swarming lemmings. Men who played presidents on TV could become presidents. The water might run out ... An evil scent would hang over the ending. And a TV star might miraculously return the love of a foolish old coot, giving him an unlikely romantic triumph which would redeem a long, small life.[1]

Rushdie's last novel *Quichotte*, synchronous with the pandemic end of the world, is a book about what? The end of the world, of course. In its last pages the world actually ends, disappears, vanishes into the void.

But the four hundred pages of the book recount much more than this.

Quichotte is an old American man of Indian birth who is the cousin and employee of Dr Smile, producer and smuggler of the deadliest drugs in the history of the United States: fentanyl and OxyContin. Big Pharma again.

Quichotte is on the brink of senile dementia, it goes without saying.

After working for years as a psycho-pharma salesman, he forgets things concerning the recent past, but to make up for it he has an unbridled imagination that is fed by countless hours of TV watching, just like the Caballero de la Triste Figura read too many adventurous books during his own historical time.

Watching TV, Quichotte has fallen in love with a new Dulcinea: a TV star of Indian origin (actually from the same city where Quichotte was born, the legendary Bombay that has since been renamed).

Quichotte is a story of broken souls, broken lives, broken bodies and broken families: the story of contemporary America and of the contemporary world at large.

'Broken families may be our best available lenses through which to view this broken world. And inside the broken families are broken people, broken by loss, poverty, maltreatment, failure, age, sickness, pain, and hatred, yet trying in spite of it all to cling to hope and love, and these broken people – we, the broken people! – may be the best mirrors of our times.'[2]

There is also Sancho of course, the young untaught man who is the imaginary son of Quichotte. He looks bewildered because the world he is supposed to inhabit is incomprehensible, probably because it is meaningless, in the sense of divested of any meaning. He is a symbol of the millennial generation that came to the world when the world was already irremediably squandered, on the brink of the final collapse.

Things fall apart as well as people. Countries fall apart as well as their citizens. A zillion channels and nothing to hold them together. Garbage out there, and great stuff out there, too, and they both coexist at the same level of reality, both give off the same air of authority. How's a young person supposed to tell them part? How to discriminate? Every show on every network tells you the same thing: based upon a true story. But that's not true either. The true story there is there's no true story anymore. There's no *true* anymore that anyone can agree on. There's a headache beginning in here. Boom! Here it is.

Ow.

What a time for me to arrive.[3]

Quichotte is a book about America, of course. The demented old protagonist is traversing the continent from California to New York and from New York to California, like his ancestor from La Mancha was traversing the wilderness of Spain. Rushdie is depicting America during the Trump years from the point of view of two dark-faced Indians, Quichotte and Sancho, who several times are aggressively treated, insulted, pushed out of restaurants and so on. People ask them where their turban is, where they have concealed their weapons, and question their right to walk into a public space.

Why are they so aggressive? Sancho asks himself. Then he realises that the problem is language, and he tells Quichotte, 'I want … to defy the bastards who hate us for possessing another tongue.'[4]

Ignorance and self-delusion of supremacy: this is the background of all kinds of racism, particularly of white American Trumpism.

While America is the most advanced place in the world in the field of research and innovation thanks to Syrians like Steve Jobs, Indians like Sundar Pichai and Rushdie himself, and Italian filmmakers and Chinese engineers, this cosmopolitan hub of intellectual labour is also the homeland of the most ignorant community of all times and places: the white colonisers.

Because of this contradiction this country is on the brink of disintegration.

'I can't look up. Up there, what is that. Like a colossus with a huge blaster blew a hole in the air. You look at it, you want to die. This can't be fixed. I don't believe there's anyone in DC or Canaveral who knows what the fuck to do about *this*.'[5]

This can't be fixed, because, 'The nothingness burst through the somethingness of the world, roaring like a fire, and then the increasingly familiar giant-bullet-hole shape was all that was left, the awe-inspiring black void of nonexistence ...'

'The voids.'[6]

Quichotte has been searching for truth, beauty, perfection and faith. He has been on the verge of realising his dream, of possessing his beloved TV star whose name is Salma, but he soon discovers that the lady is not interested in him but rather in the opioid drugs that he has in his suitcase, and that this drug can buy her benevolence, but it is also going to kill her.

'Perhaps ... only at the end of the quest did the seeker understand how deeply rooted in error his journey had been.'[7]

So Quichotte reaches the end of his journey as an essentially tragic character. As Miguel de Unamuno has observed about the work of Cervantes, it explores the way in which we are sometimes overwhelmed by our mortality – not death, as such, but something worse, a sense of being annihilated, a supreme anguish.

'Can nothing be done to reverse the decay?' asks Salma, the heroin-addicted bipolar protagonist of the mediascape.

And Dr Evel Cent (a name that sounds like Evil Scent) replies:

'I am the last Cassandra of the human story.'[8]

Forget about Quichotte, now we are going to speak about delusions of the end.

Baudrillard knew that the end is an illusion, a form of trepidation, a never-ending wait.

The last utopia.

The end of what?

Slavoj Žižek says that it's easier to imagine the end of the world than the end of capitalism.

But Deleuze and Guattari say that a rhizome has no beginning and no end, it is always in the middle.

In the metaphysical sphere of Being, and in the dialectical sphere of historical teleology, *end* means an overcoming and emergence of the new.

But as we leave the metaphysical kingdom there is no end, only recombinations of information and recompositions of matter.

Let's understand the distinction between the end of a shape and the end of a body.

Bodies finish when they decompose; but matter does not vanish, it does not become Nothingness, it only recomposes in new forms, in new molecular configurations.

Shape, on the contrary, exists only in the mind, which is a generator of perception.

Shape can vanish and become Nothingness, as consciousness dissolves.

Consciousness in fact is the condition of Nothingness. Nothingness can exist only as the becoming-nothing of a consciousness, as a dissolution and final shutting down of consciousness.

When a form grows unable to organise content, at that point the content turns into chaos, and the mind perceives chaos as a painful spasm. Then the mind projects a new form, and the world can be recomposed. But the mind itself dissolves when finally the matter composing the body loses consistency. Although the body does not fall into Nothingness thanks to the eternal becoming of decomposable matter, it's the body that causes the dissolution of the mind, and the following emergence of Nothingness.

There is no Nothingness but the becoming-nothing of consciousness.

Only in the mind Nothingness dwells.

Only projecting Nothingness can the book find its end, because it is interminable.

Only the dissolution of the body of a thinking mind can generate Nothingness.

The end of language is nothing: and nothing is also the subsumption of language by the automaton, the soulless and bodiless language.

The increasing replacement of human language by the automatic language of the evolving machine enables the great awakening of Nothingness as artificial intelligence. The increasing translation of conjunctive word with a code. The generation of automatic signs whose meaning is established by the code. Automated signification is nothing.

The world does not disappear when my mind stops thinking it, because the world is nothing, and it goes on, it continues its evolution in the dimension of Nothingness (of 'my' Nothingness, in fact).

The Hindu legend recounts that God fell asleep for a while, and during that instant the world emerged and took shape, and in that world dreamed by God during that moment of unconsciousness the history of men did unfold.

The history of men, but what about the history of women?

Contrary to what I said before (the world is nothing), the world really exists because the feminine body withdraws from God, does not trust God, and feminine atheism makes the world enjoyable, joyful and therefore true.

We may, however, theorise another hypothesis.

After an extremely long existence (some say eternal), God happened to be hit by Alzheimer's disease, that kind of senile dementia that follows an irreversible degradation of brain tissues.

He loses the memory of his dreams, of his errors, of his creations. He loses memory of us, so we are left alone.

The Alzheimer of God has already been described as Kali Yuga. God forgets who He is. To the question *Who are you?* he could answer, *A pensioner at the post office, waiting for my turn in the queue.*

Kali, the sombre mate of Siva, has been tyrannising the world since the moment of the physical death of Krishna (which happened, according to the Surya Siddhanta, at midnight on

18 February 3102 before Christ), and the tyranny of Kali will last only 432,000 years, and will conclude in the year 428,899 after Christ. Kalki, the tenth and last avatar of Vishnu, will appear in that year on a white horse with a flaming sword that will dissipate evil.

So we have to wait until the year 428,899 after Christ, when the Age of Kali the great destroyer will end.

Kali, the Alzheimer of God.

There are many Gods in this story: the constantly awakened and quite nervous God of the Bible, the sleeping God of Buddhist legend, and the crazy God of the Hindus.

Totally incomprehensible is the stubbornness of humans in continuing at every price an experiment that has largely proved to be a failure.

While the unconscious God dreams of the world as he falls asleep, Abraham's God is always hyperexcited, taking amphetamine and sometimes going too far in his madness.

When dementia took possession of his senescent brain, tired of such a long existence he gave way to the history of men.

That is now drawing to a close.

Or maybe not.

Notes

1. Threshold/Poetry

1 William S. Burroughs, *The Ticket That Exploded* (New York: Grove Press, 1987), p. 49.

2 Paolo Virno, *Saggio Sulla Negazione* (Turin: Bollati Boringhieri, 2013).

3 William Burroughs, *The Place of Dead Roads* (New York: Holt, Rinehart and Winston, 1983), p. 155.

4 William Burroughs, 'Astronaut's Return,' in *Exterminator!* (New York: Viking, 1973), p. 24.

5 Daniel Odier, *The Job: Interviews with William S. Burroughs* (New York: Grove Press, 1974), p. 27.

6 Salman Rushdie, *Quichotte: A Novel* (New York: Random House, 2019), p. 258.

2. Beyond the Breakdown

1 Giorgio Agamben, 'Lo stato d'eccezione provocato da un'emergenza immotivata', *il manifesto* (26 February 2020) and 'Quando la casa brucia', *Quodlibet* (5 October 2020).

3. Semiotics of the Virus

1 Gabriel Eira and Nicolás Guigou, 'De virus, capitalismo analógico y virtual', *Hemisferio izquierdo* (25 April 2020), hemisferio izquierdo.uy. My translation.

2 Eira and Guigou, 'De virus'.

4. The Spectrum and the Horizon

1 Quoted in Plato, *Thaetetus* (London: Penguin, 1987), p. 30.

2 Carlo Rovelli, *The Order of Time* (New York: Penguin Books, 2018).

5. Psycho-systemic Collapse

1 'Riding on the Dynamic of Disaster: An Interview with Robert Fripp', by Allan Jones, *Melody Maker*, April 28, 1979.

6. Freedom and Potency

1 William James, *The Thought and Character of William James*, vol. 1 (Boston, Little, Brown, 1936), p. 323

7. Unconscious/*Verdrängung*

1 Friedrich Schelling, *System of Transcendental Idealism*, 1800.
2 Sigmund Freud, *Opere* (Rome: Gruppo Editoriale, 2006), pp. 499–595. My translation.
3 Ignacio Matte Blanco, *The Unconscious as Infinite Sets* (London: Gerald Duckworth, 1975), p. 17.
4 Carl Jung, *Über die Psychologie des Unbewussten* (Zurich: Rascher Verlag, 1943), p. 67. My translation.
5 Ibid.
6 Freud, *Opere*.
7 Donna Haraway, *Staying with the Trouble: Making Kin in the Chthulucene* (Durham, NC: Duke University Press, 2016), p. 130.
8 Ibid., p. 58.

8. Autistic Mindscape

1 Patrick Barkham, 'Natural Talent: The 16-Year-Old Writer Taking the World by Storm' (includes an interview with Dara McAnulty), *Guardian*, 16 May 2020.
2 Barkham, 'Natural Talent'.
3 'Autism Spectrum Disorder', National Institute of Mental Health, nimh.nih.gov.
4 Gloria Steinem, introduction to *Parable of the Sower*, by Octavia E. Butler (New York: Seven Stories Press, 2017), p. v, first published 1993.
5 Butler, *Parable of the Sower*.

9. XXX

1 Julie Gordon, 'Wear a Mask While Having Sex, Canada's Top Doctor Suggests', Reuters, 2 September 2020, reuters.com.
2 'Casual Sex Is Out, Companionship Is In,' *Economist*, 9 May 2020.
3 Nayeema Raza, 'What Single People Are Starting to Realize', *New York Times*, 18 May 2020.

4 Raza, 'Single People'.
5 Peter Ueda et al., 'Trends in Frequency of Sexual Activity and Number of Sexual Partners Among Adults Aged 18 to 44 Years in the US, 2000–2018', *JAMA Network Open* 3/6, June 2020.
6 Haraway, *Staying with the Trouble*, pp. 6, 7.
7 Albert Camus, *Le mythe de Sisyphe* (Paris: Éditions Gallimard, 2020), p. 165. My translation.

10. Sad Is Eros
1 W. H. Auden, 'In Memory of Sigmund Freud', in *Another Time* (New York: Random House, 1940).
2 'Statistics on Daily Gun Violence in America', bradyunited.org.
3 Auden, 'Sigmund Freud'.
4 Ciara Gaffney, 'Sex During Lockdown: Are We Witnessing a Cybersexual Revolution?', *Guardian*, 20 April 2020.
5 Gaffney, 'Sex During Lockdown'.
6 Ibid.
7 Julie Halpert, 'How to Manage Panic Attacks', *New York Times*, 11 April 2020.

11. Mythology of the End
1 Ernesto De Martino, *La fine del mondo* (Milan: Giulio Einaudi, 2019), p. 70. My translation.
2 Wretched of the Earth, 'An Open Letter to Extinction Rebellion', *Common Dreams*, 4 May 2019, commondreams.org.
3 De Martino, *La fine del mondo*, p. 355.
4 Margaret Thatcher, interview by Douglas Keay, *Woman's Own*, 31 Oct. 1987, available at Margaret Thatcher Foundation, margaretthatcher.org/.
5 The Doors, 'The End', *The Doors* (Elektra, 1967).

12. Questioning Senility
1 Erika Hayasaki, 'Has this Scientist Finally Found the Fountain of Youth?,' *MIT Technology Review* 122/5, Sep.–Oct. 2019.
2 David Adam, 'What if Aging Weren't Inevitable, but a Curable Disease?' *MIT Technology Review* 122/5, Sep.–Oct. 2019.
3 Ibid.
4 Ibid.
5 Arthur Schnitzler, 'Casanova's Homecoming', in *Plays and Stories: Arthur Schnitzler* (New York: Continuum, 1982), p. 184.

6   Henri Bianchi, foreword to *La question du vieillissement* (Paris: Dunod, 1989), pp. 3–4. My translation.
7   Marta Kowalska et al., abstract to 'Aging and Neurological Diseases', in *Senescence: Physiology or Pathology*, eds. Jolanta Dorszewska and Wojciech Kozubski (London: IntechOpen, 2017), p. 63.

13. Making Friends with Death

1   Philippe Ariès, *Essais sur l'histoire de la mort en Occident du moyen âge à nos jours* (Paris: Le Seuil, 2014), p. 129. My translation.
2   Epicurus, 'Principle Doctrines', quoted in Diogenes Laertius, *The Lives of the Eminent Philosophers* (New York: Oxford University Press, 2018) p. 538.
3   James Hillman, *Il suicidio e l'anima* (New York: Harper & Row, 1964), p. 30. My translation.
4   James Hillman, *The Force of Character: And the Lasting Life* (New York: Random House, 1999), p. 6.

14. Pleasure and Desire

1   Plato, *Theages*, in *Plato in Twelve Volumes*, vol. 8, trans. W. R. M. Lamb (Cambridge, MA: Harvard University Press, 1955), 130d–130e.
2   Deleuze letter, in Paolo Godani, *Sul piacere che manca: Etica del desiderio e spirito del capitalismo* (Rome: DeriveApprodi, 2019), p. 74. My translation.
3   Paolo Godani, *Sul piacere che manca: Etica del desiderio e spirito del capitalism* (Rome: DeriveApprodi, 2019), p. 36. My translation.
4   Ibid.

15. Exhaustion

1   Lawrence H. Summers, 'The Age of Secular Stagnation', *Foreign Affairs* 95/2 (March/April 2016), pp. 2–9.
2   Haraway, *Staying with the Trouble*, pp. 3–4.
3   Greta Thunberg, address to the general assembly of the United Nations Climate Action Summit (United Nations: New York, 23 September 2019).
4   Wretched of the Earth, speech at the London Climate Strike, 20 September 2019.

5 Sara Aridi, 'Capernaum Is Not Just a Film, but a Rallying Cry' (includes an interview with Nadine Labaki), *New York Times*, 14 December 2018.

16. The American Insurrection as Preventive Psychotherapy

1 Daniella Adeluwoye: 'Under-25s Bearing Brunt of Covid Mental-Health Toll – Survey', *Guardian*, 30 August 2020.
2 Ibid.
3 Halpert, 'How to Manage Panic Attacks'.

17. Nothingness – the Alzheimer's of God

1 Salman Rushdie, *Quichotte* (New York: Random House, 2020), pp. 7–8.
2 Ibid., pp. 54–5.
3 Ibid., p. 133.
4 Ibid., p. 151.
5 Ibid., p. 374.
6 Ibid., pp. 377, 379.
7 Ibid., p. 381.
8 Ibid., p. 384.